More MONTANA MOMENTS

Ellen Baumler

MONTANA HISTORICAL SOCIETY
HELENA, MONTANA

Cover: *Laugh Kills Lonesome* (detail), by Charles M. Russell (oil on canvas, 1925, 18"h x 30"w), Montana Historical Society, Helena, Mackay Collection, X1955.01.01

Cover and book design by Diane Gleba Hall
Typeset in FF Scala and Gill Sans
Printed in the United States

Distributed by Globe Pequot Press, 246 Goose Lane, Guilford, CT 06437
(800) 243-0495

12 13 14 15 16 17 18 19 20   10 9 8 7 6 5 4 3 2 1

Library of Congress Cataloging-in-Publication Data
Baumler, Ellen.
More Montana moments / Ellen Baumler.
     p. cm.
Includes index.

ISBN 978-0-9801292-6-7 (pbk. : alk. paper)

1. Montana—History. 2. Montana—Biography. I. Title.
     F731.B384 2012
     978.6—dc23

                                   2012016609

Contents

ix   Foreword

I   Through the Artists' Eyes

11   An Eclectic Sense of Place

21   More than Just a Home

30   Rest in Peace

45   Legal and Illegal Capers

59   Homesteading Tales

68   Bless the Beasts

76   And the Children

87   Educating and Correcting Youth

96   What They Left Behind

108   The Good, the Bad, and Otherwise

124   On the Home Front and Abroad

135   Medical Missteps and Milestones

144   Holidays Remembered

156   Legends and Treasures of the Treasure State

165   From Steamboats to Skunkwagons

176   Impressing Visitors Then and Now

186   Mining's Boom and Bust

197   Modernizing Montana

Illustrations

x   *Laugh Kills Lonesome,* by Charles M. Russell

27   Greenough Mansion, Missoula

34   William Wesley "Brother Van" Van Orsdel at Greenfield wedding

52   Edith Colby mugshot

61   Grace Binks and Margaret Majors at homestead shack near Sumatra

64   Buckley sister in divided skirt

71   Charlie Russell on his favorite horse, Monte

83   Elizabeth Farmer with mother and sister at Bearmouth

94   University of Montana students painting the M

103   Pictograph Cave

110   Crow Chief Plenty Coups

117   "Daddy" Reeves and the harmonica choir of the Montana Deaconess School

127   Italian seamen on work release from Fort Missoula

130   Twenty-fifth Infantry bicycle corps at Mammoth Hot Springs

136   St. Mary's Mission, Father Ravalli's cabin, and visiting Salish

151   Rio Theatre, Helena

159   Mission Canyon, Little Rockies

172   Cromwell Dixon and the *Hummingbird,* his plane

183   Earthquake Lake

191   Hydraulic placer mining

198   Virginia City street scene

202   President Franklin Roosevelt at Fort Peck Dam site

Foreword

༃ *Montana Moments: History on the Go,* published in 2010, was
the product of several years' worth of ninety-second radio
scripts compiled for my *History Half-Notes* radio show at Helena's
KCAP AM. In 2011, the program reemerged on Cherry Creek Radio's
KBLL 1240 AM in Helena. The new program followed *History Half-
Notes*'s same format, but the length increased from ninety seconds
to two minutes per program, airing five days a week under the new
title *History on the Go.* Thus readers will notice slightly longer entries
in *More Montana Moments.*

As with *Montana Moments,* the scripts in this collection reflect
diverse research. Some of it has been accomplished in my job at the
Montana Historical Society as coordinator for Montana's National
Register sign program. Properties listed in the National Register of
Historic Places in this book are so noted with an asterisk in their
first mention. Bits and pieces of the many articles and books I have
researched and written on diverse subjects have also made their way
into entries here. Readers familiar with my work elsewhere may
notice familiar themes and threads.

More Montana Moments is the accumulation of scripts from
April 2011 to April 2012. Cherry Creek Radio, my enthusiastic
Helena listeners of all ages, the Montana Historical Society Press,
and Society director Bruce Whittenberg have made this sequel to
Montana Moments possible. I wish to thank them and my boss, Kirby
Lambert, in the Outreach and Interpretation program. Thanks also
to my colleagues at the Montana Historical Society and to editor
Christy Goll, for their help and support in this endeavor.

—ELLEN BAUMLER

Laugh Kills Lonesome, by Charles M. Russell (oil on canvas, 1925, 18"h x 30"w)

Through the Artists' Eyes

Laugh Kills Lonesome

ARTIST Charles Marion Russell carefully chose the subjects of his art based on personal experience. He, more than any other western artist, painted what he knew with great longing and nostalgia for the cowboy way of life he lived and loved so well. In 1925, a year before his death, Russell painted *Laugh Kills Lonesome*, a tribute to this vanishing cowboy lifestyle. The painting depicts an evening campfire scene, one that Russell probably recalled from his youth. He painted himself into the picture as an old cowpoke stopping by the warm and friendly circle for a cup of coffee and a hearty laugh at the end of a long day in the saddle. The title has been hailed as fine as the painting, and several contemporary artists have used it and further interpreted Russell's famous scene. One of these is poet Mike Logan. Another is musician-songwriter Michael Nesmith of the 1960s pop rock group the Monkees. Nesmith went on to a stellar career as a songwriter and musician. His insightful, lyrical song "Laugh Kills Lonesome" plays upon the universal camaraderie of humor. His lyrics tell the story that Russell meant to convey. The lyrics read in part:

> All around the campfire stood seven dusty men
> The cook was drinking applejack, the cattle were all penned

Someone must have cracked a wise one because the men began
　　to grin
Their smiles shot out like sunbeams and made the night give in
Because
Laugh kills lonesome every single time
That's why Charlie Russell painted it
And why it looks so fine
Laugh kills lonesome every single time.

And Nesmith's lyrics still ring as true as the subject of Russell's painting.

Hard Winter

THE hard winter of 1886–87 changed ranching practices forever. Thousands of head of livestock, grazing unchecked on the open range, did not survive. The winter was brutally cold and did take a toll, but stock had survived cold weather before. However, unusual periods of freeze and thaw, one after another, robbed the spring grass of nutrients, and cattle continued to starve even after the weather warmed. Ranching practices were another problem. Montana herds had become so vast that a true count was not possible; the big ranchers really didn't know how many head of livestock they had at any given time. This devastating winter wiped out many a large outfit. Louis Stadler and Louis Kaufman, partners in the OH Ranch near Utica, asked their cowboys how the stock was faring. The answer came from a young cowhand named Charlie Russell in the form of a sketch of a starving cow with waiting wolves circling him. Russell called it *Waiting for a Chinook* or *The Last of the 5,000*. Granville Stuart, of the huge DHS Ranch, vowed that he would never again own an animal he could not shelter and feed. Ranchers began to fence the range, manage much smaller herds, store winter feed, and build huge barns. The Kleffner Ranch barn south of East Helena is one example. Ranch founder W. C. Child built the cavernous fieldstone barn in 1887 to hold at least 500 head of cattle and 250 tons of hay. It and other large Montana barns built to shelter many animals recall that devastating winter when so many perished.

Ralph DeCamp

CHARLIE RUSSELL, Edgar S. Paxson, and Ralph DeCamp make up the great triumvirate of Montana's best-loved frontier artists. All three contributed to the art in the Montana State Capitol and were great friends. Although DeCamp was also a fine photographer and portrait painter, he is best known for his landscapes. DeCamp spent his teen years in Moorehead, Minnesota, the terminus of the Northern Pacific Railroad. He studied at the Pennsylvania School of Art and then, back at Moorehead, got a big break when he sketched a train accident he had witnessed. His drawings, as evidence in court, drew the attention of a high-ranking railroad official. The Northern Pacific hired DeCamp to join a group of artists painting and photographing Yellowstone National Park. This was a huge opportunity as train stations displayed original artwork and were Montana's first art galleries. DeCamp fell in love with Montana's landscape potential and soon moved to Helena. There, painting the Gates of the Mountains, he met Margaret Hilger, daughter of a prominent rancher. They married and were a good match. Margaret was a renowned violinist, and she accompanied her husband on his countryside excursions, practicing her violin as he painted. Charlie Russell said that DeCamp painted the wettest water he had ever seen, so wet you could hear it ripple. Consequently, he always had more buyers for his art than he had paintings. After Margaret died suddenly in 1934, DeCamp went to live in Chicago with his son, bought a car, and continued painting the countryside until his death in 1936. DeCamp's work is rarely for sale because those who own his paintings cherish them.

Driving the Golden Spike

THE most visible art in the Montana State Capitol attests to the importance of the arrival of the Northern Pacific Railroad. *Driving the Golden Spike* commemorates the great event that took place at Gold Creek on September 8, 1883, marking the completion of the last section of track across the vast stretches of the state. While Governor Joseph K. Toole oversaw the subjects of the Capitol's other art, the Northern Pacific insisted upon the right to dictate the subject matter and the people depicted in this painting. Railroad officials chose as the artist Amédée Joullin, who earned his credentials as an artist at the Ecole des Beaux-Arts and the Académie Julian in Paris. Finished in 1903, the oil on canvas was unveiled first in California and subsequently mounted in its place of honor at the top of the grand stairway beneath the stained glass barrel vault in the Capitol. It is indeed impressive in its place of honor. In consultation with railroad officials, Joullin drew on photographs of the event and portraits of the participants to create the mural. Former U.S. president Ulysses S. Grant holds the sledgehammer while Northern Pacific president Henry Villard looks on. A delegation of Crow Indians, whose land the railroad crossed, includes Chief Iron Bull. Generic onlookers include soldiers, cowboys, miners, and railroad men. Absent, however, are those who actually did the work laying the tracks across Montana: the Irish, the Chinese, and other laborers. The golden spike used in the ceremony was not actually gold at all but a working iron spike that reputedly was used to begin the transcontinental project in Minnesota in 1872.

Edgar S. Paxson

BELOVED Montana artist Edgar S. Paxson was the son of Quaker parents. His father was a painter of theatrical scenery. Like his fellow artist Charlie Russell, Paxson came west looking for adventure. He arrived in Montana in 1877 and like Russell worked as a wrangler, cow punching, scouting, and hunting for his cattlemen bosses. Paxson's life experiences on the range gave him subject matter, but he put his own twist on history. He knew and interviewed many of the characters he later depicted and carefully painted them as he wanted them to be, not always as they really were. For example, Paxson knew the great Salish chief Charlo. His painting of the Salish exodus from the Bitterroot Valley, *The Flatheads Leaving Their Bitterroot Home, October, 1892,* portrays finely dressed warriors brandishing rifles. In reality, the Salish were a poor and broken people forced out of their homeland. Paxson settled in Butte in 1880, painting signs and theatrical scenery to support his family. Paxson was entirely self-taught like Russell, but he lacked the marketing opportunities and exposure that Russell gained from his wife Nancy's determined salesmanship. The Spanish-American War intervened with Paxson's career, and he and his son Harry together volunteered for service. En route home, the ship encountered a typhoon, and a wave slammed Paxson against a spar, causing serious internal injuries from which he never recovered. But despite his feeble health, he moved to Missoula and, driven by his art, worked until the day he died in 1919, leaving a wonderful legacy. His most famous work, *Custer's Last Stand,* is in the Buffalo Bill Historical Center in Cody, Wyoming. In Montana, Paxson's murals grace the Montana State Capitol and the Missoula County Courthouse.

State Capitol Rotunda Roundels

THE Pedretti brothers painted much of the art in the Montana State Capitol, but it was Governor Joseph K. Toole who dictated the subject matter. Toole wanted the Capitol to reflect the people and events important to Montana's heritage. In the magnificent Capitol's rotunda, four roundels, painted on canvas in 1902, portray people important to Montana's past. *The Trapper* represents famous mountain man Jim Bridger (1804–81), who guided many early trappers and explorers into the Montana wilderness. The portrait acknowledges the trappers and explorers who paved the way for the first white settlers. *The Indian Chief* represents the Salish chief Charlo (1830–1910), who resisted the removal of his people from the Bitterroot Valley to the Jocko Reservation. Whether Governor Toole meant to emphasize Charlo's resistance to government authority or his final acquiescence poses an interesting question. *The Prospector* commemorates those who exploited Montana's mineral wealth with pickax and gold pan. The portrait represents Henry Edgar, one of the six discoverers of Alder Gulch. Edgar became a respected member of the early community and lends a special dignity to the image of the rough miner. Cowboys were already romanticized as a dying breed by 1902, but they provided the foundation for the huge cattle industry that brought immense wealth to Montana. Governor Toole suggested that the Pedrettis study the cowboys in Charlie Russell's paintings for inspiration for *The Cowboy*. The cowboy is the only anonymous figure among the four roundels.

John L. Clarke

ARTIST J. K. Ralston said that when John L. Clarke finished carving a bear, you could smell it. Clarke was a gifted wood carver, highly celebrated in his own lifetime. John D. Rockefeller even purchased eight of his carvings. The grandson of trader Malcolm Clarke and his Piegan wife, John Clarke was three-quarters Blackfeet. His grandfather Malcolm was killed in 1869 over a dispute with his in-laws. His father, Horace, was shot through the head during that incident but recovered. When Clarke was a toddler, scarlet fever claimed five of his brothers and left him profoundly deaf. He was sent away to schools for the deaf in the 1890s and educated at North Dakota and at Montana's state school at Boulder. There he learned wood carving. Clarke mostly communicated through sign language and was known by his Blackfeet name, Catapuis, which means the Man Who Talks Not. Despite his handicap, Clarke was highly gifted, largely self-taught, and spent most of his life carving spectacular wildlife at his studio in East Glacier. His work includes clay sculpture, paintings, sketches, and the famed mountain goat insignia of the Great Northern Railway. His last work was a carving of a grizzly bear freeing itself from a trap. Clarke did this remarkable carving almost entirely by feel, his ninety-year-old eyes so clouded with cataracts that he could hardly see. Clarke's work has been exhibited throughout the United States and in London, England. President Warren G. Harding commissioned an eagle holding an American flag that he displayed in the Oval Office during his presidency. The John L. Clarke Western Art Gallery and Memorial Museum in East Glacier commemorates the work of this exceptional artist who was one of Montana's finest native sons.

Painted Tipis

SINGING VOICE, of the Gros Ventre people, recounted this story of painted tipis to her daughter-in-law Katie Long Horse. Singing Voice explained that painted tipis were common among the Plains tribes. Medicine people and spiritual warriors owned these very special lodges. They were of all colors and designs. Each unique tipi displayed the sacred design and colors of that particular spiritual leader. These designs were passed down from father to son and always stayed in that clan or tribe. Many of these tipis existed among the Gros Ventres, and the design always followed the same pattern. At the bottom of the tipi, an encircling band of dark color represented Mother Earth. Within this band, a row of circles, called dusty stars, depicted meteors that had fallen to the earth. Next, a row of rounded or sharp projections symbolized mountain ridges or peaks. Upon the broad central part of the tipi was a unique animal, bird, sacred rock, or thunder trail representing the owner's sacred medicine, and it was this that gave the lodge its protective power. At the top around the ears of the flaps, a broad circle of black represented the night sky. The sun and crescent moon were often painted on top as well as the Seven Sisters of the Big Dipper and the Lost Children of the Great Bear. The cross on top of the tipi represented the morning star and also symbolized the butterfly or sleep bringer whose great power brought good dreams to the owner. Painted tipis, according to Singing Voice, always had the same designs no matter what. The people respected their owners and never copied another's tipi.

Ledger Art

PICTOGRAPHS on cliff faces and cave walls are the first artworks of Montana's native people. As guns and horses were introduced in the mid-1700s, pictographs begin to portray these items, reflecting dramatic changes in Indian lifeways. Unlike their ancient counterparts, these paintings also begin to depict recognizable events. Animal skins, especially buffalo hides, were also vehicles for art and a way of reckoning time or recording important events. With the demise of the buffalo and other game animals, Indian artists transferred their artwork to other materials, such as muslin, paper, canvas, and sometimes cowhide. This art form, called ledger art because of the adaptation to small-size paper in the form of ledger books, is a transition between the pre-reservation period and the later Native American painting styles that emerged in the 1920s. Ledger art reflects the availability of different art materials, such as crayons, pencils, commercial paints, and brushes. These new materials replaced stick brushes and natural paints made from native plants, minerals, and bone. Ledger art continued the tradition of telling the story of a person's life and exploits. Stylistic differences can reveal the tribe of the artist. For example, Crow artists painted elongated figures to show movement, while in Blackfeet art, multiple hoofprints showed the horse's forward movement. Several pieces of ledger art in the Montana Historical Society's extensive collection poignantly illustrate the life and exploits of Elk Head, a Gros Ventre inmate at the Montana Territorial Penitentiary in the 1880s. Drawing on paper with pencil, Elk Head depicts one scene showing himself as a baby on his mother's back while an enemy Sioux fires his rifle at her. Ledger art provides exceptional documentation of Indian experiences and illustrates the dramatic cultural changes white encroachment and reservations imposed.

Bill Stockton's Chief Joseph

BILL STOCKTON was a sheepman and artist who returned to Montana after World War II to settle on his family ranch near Grass Range. Art and sheep seem an odd combination, but Stockton's tender heart, love for his animals, and closeness to the land provided a lifetime of inspiration. His legacy includes writings, sketches, paintings, and sculpture. Stockton found the plight of Chief Joseph and the Nez Perces, who tried unsuccessfully to flee from the U.S. Army to sanctuary in Canada, extremely troubling. So in the 1950s he created a haunting metal sculpture known as *Chief Joseph*. It depicts a head with arms upraised in poignant recapitulation. Stockton sent the piece to an art retailer in Billings. Thieves broke into the business and stole the sculpture and several other pieces of Stockton's work. A year later, a young Indian man allegedly committed suicide by jumping off a bridge into the Yellowstone River. As Yellowstone County officials dragged the river looking for him, they not only recovered the young man's body but also discovered Stockton's sculpture of Chief Joseph. It had been in the river for a year. It was as if the spirit of the young man aided in the recovery of the artwork. The sculpture later was entered in the Great Falls Russell Art Show and Auction, where journalist Kay Hansen saw it. She knew she had to have the piece. With only nine dollars in her pocket, Hansen bid and acquired the sculpture, paying for it in monthly installments. She has recently donated it to the Montana Historical Society. It is one of Stockton's most important creations.

Elizabeth Lochrie

THE U.S. Treasury Department, the State of Montana, the Ford Motor Company, New York Life Insurance Company, and the First National Bank of Seattle were among the distinguished patrons of Deer Lodge native Elizabeth Lochrie. Formally trained as an artist at the Pratt Institute in New York City, she graduated in 1911 and settled in Butte. From the 1920s to the 1950s, Lochrie established herself as a fine portrait artist. She also painted local rural and urban landscapes and scenes. During 1924 and 1925, Lochrie painted eighteen children's murals for the Montana State Hospital at Galen. She also created murals for several post office buildings. In 1937, Lochrie won the U.S. Treasury Department's competition for *News from the States* at the Dillon Post Office, depicting the historic arrival of mail in that community. At Glacier National Park, Lochrie studied under Winold Reiss and then served as artist for the Great Northern Railway from 1937 to 1939. While other artists documented the vanishing Indian lifeway, Lochrie did more than that. She immersed herself in Indian culture and learned to converse in various dialects. She traveled the lecture circuit and often used her fees to buy clothing and other items for needy tribal members, especially Blackfeet. In 1932, the Blackfeet Nation adopted her and named her *Netchitaki*, Woman Alone in Her Way. When she died in 1981, Lochrie left a legacy of more than one thousand paintings, murals, and sculptures. She was one of Montana's most outstanding twentieth-century artists.

An Eclectic Sense of Place

National Register of Historic Places

MONTANA'S heritage is important to everyone—after all, how can you know where you are going if you don't know where you have been? Montana has hundreds of special places honored with listing in the National Register of Historic Places. But the intent of this National Park Service–administered program is poorly understood. Created by the Historic Preservation Act in 1966, the register was designed to recognize places important to national, state, and/or local history and worthy of preservation. Contrary to what many believe, register listing does not guarantee preservation or protection of any property. Listing does, however, raise public awareness and in certain cases allows commercial property owners to apply for federal tax credits. Common myths include the notion that listed properties cannot be insured. This is entirely false. The idea that owners of listed properties must open their homes to the public is also a common belief. No property owner is ever under such an obligation. Finally, the idea that owners of listed properties cannot change or even demolish them is not the case. However, sometimes there are restrictions on historic properties at the local level. For example, Virginia City*, Montana, has approved stringent local ordinances that can affect commercial and residential buildings. Register listing requires historical research and submission of a nomination form and photographs to the state review board, which meets three times annually. Board-approved nominations are then sent to the Keeper of the National Register in Washington, D.C., for the final determination. The State Historic Preservation Office, under the auspices of the Montana Historical Society, coordinates Montana's National Register program. Hundreds of buildings and sites across the state have been honored with National Register listing.

*Placer Hotel**

ARTIST Charlie Russell illustrated the program for the formal ball, held April 12, 1913, inaugurating the largest hotel between the Twin Cities and the Coast. Built almost entirely with donations as a public enterprise, the Placer Hotel quickly became the center of civic activity, and Helena felt real pride of ownership. Its name derives from the placer gold washed from the gravel during the excavation of its foundation. As the foundation was being dug, an old-timer prospector was called in to demonstrate the art of panning. Soon he had a crowd fascinated with the lesson. Legend has it that in digging the basement, workers found enough gold to pay for the building and then some. Architect George H. Carsley designed the grand hotel in consultation with Cass Gilbert, architect of New York's famed Woolworth Building. The Placer's wrought-iron balconies, overhanging eaves, and wide cornice are reminiscent of the nearby Montana Club*, designed by Gilbert in 1905. The seven-story hotel was constructed of reinforced concrete and brick from the Western Clay Manufacturing Company*, which is now the Archie Bray Foundation. Each of its 172 guest rooms, arranged around a U-shape, opened onto the outside. Custom-made china, cutlery, and bed linens—supplied by Helena's New York Store—all bore the hotel's prospector insignia. The hotel featured a carriage entrance, a lobby fireplace built to burn seven-foot logs, and a state-of-the-art kitchen with an automatic dishwasher and a central refrigeration system. The Placer, which once welcomed a campaigning John F. Kennedy as a guest, is now divided into condominiums.

Anaconda Saddle Club*

COPPER KING Marcus Daly built a racetrack outside his company town of Anaconda in 1888. The track promoted his passion for horse racing and added a venue for his own fine Bitterroot Stock Farm thoroughbreds. The racetrack not only offered recreational opportunities but also established the first equine activities in Anaconda's West Valley. Although modern housing obliterated Daly's racetrack in the early twentieth century, its legacy endured. The nonprofit Anaconda Saddle Club, founded in 1944 during World War II, was an extension of the tradition Daly brought to the valley. The club fostered the community's enthusiasm for horses and horsemanship at a time when resources were scarce. In 1945, the group purchased thirty acres of land and Martin Nelson and Charles Nicely volunteered as architects. Almost every evening and on Sundays during 1945 and 1946, the 160 club members worked on the construction of the oval racetrack, arena, numerous barns, and other buildings. Completion of the rustic-style complex was a great achievement by an all-volunteer workforce. A huge crowd attended the public opening on September 22, 1946. The unique octagonal clubhouse, log caretaker's house, frame buildings with weatherboard siding, and complementary log fences and corrals reflect a style unusual for the postwar period. The log building methods mirror those employed in the Anaconda Company's logging camps in the Seeley-Swan area and Flathead Valley. The club's log buildings also provide a visual connection to the rustic-style dude ranches of an earlier era. The club continues its careful stewardship of equine traditions in this superb setting, offering an excellent venue for local and regional events.

J. C. Adams Stone Barn*

THE beautiful J. C. Adams Barn in Cascade County's fertile Sun River Valley is a monument to early stock raising. The area attracted twenty-six-year-old, Kentucky-born James C. Adams, whose worldly experience belied his youth. Orphaned at ten and a Civil War prisoner at sixteen, he came to Montana at eighteen in 1864, already a seasoned teamster. Adams made a fortune working as a wagon boss for Fort Benton's Diamond R freighting outfit. In 1874, he bought property along the Sun River near Fort Shaw*. He figured soldiers would provide a ready beef market. Adams's cattle business flourished, and he soon needed more room. In 1882, he hired Swedish stonecutters to build a barn. They carved sandstone blocks from a nearby quarry and hauled them by buckboard. Completed in 1885, the barn cost an astounding ten thousand dollars. Its triple-sectioned first floor housed horses and tack; winter shelter for cattle, wagons, and buggies; and a meat locker for butchered beef. An open buckle meant welcome, and Adams chose that symbol as his brand. His hospitality became legendary. The huge hayloft accommodated many a traveler and saw roller-skating parties and community dances. Adams died in 1913, and subsequent owners have kept the landmark barn in constant use. Upon the barn's completion, the *Sun River Press* commented that it looked as if it could withstand the "storm and decay of a century at least." Thanks to careful stewardship, it has.

Pekin Noodle Parlor*

BUTTE once had Montana's largest Chinese settlement. Dwellings, club rooms, laundries, restaurants, and stores selling Chinese goods crowded its thoroughfares and alleyways. The Pekin Noodle Parlor, still a popular Butte eatery, is a lone survivor displaying Asian roots. G. E. DeSnell designed the building on speculation for Butte attorney F. T. McBride. When the building was finished in 1909, Hum Yow moved his Mercury Street noodle parlor to the second floor and soon owned the property. Upstairs noodle parlors were common in urban Chinese communities, and the Pekin's central stair and neon sign long beckoned customers. Close proximity to Butte's once-teeming red-light district has fueled local legends about the Pekin's curtained booths. However, these booths were a fixture in Asian restaurants and simply offered diners privacy. The two ground-floor storefronts housed Hum Yow's Chinese Goods and Silks and G. P. Meinhart's sign painting business. Hum Yow and his wife, Bessie Wong—both California-born, first-generation Chinese—raised three children in the rear living quarters. The Hums retired to California in 1952, and several more generations of the family have maintained this landmark business. Although Hum Yow opened his noodle parlor at this location in 1909, it became the Pekin Noodle Parlor two years later, in 1911, and has operated under that name ever since. The Pekin celebrated its one hundredth year in business in 2011.

Ismay Jail*

Ismay's bustling businesses, wicked ways, and itinerant population of cowboys and railroad men earned it the nickname "Little Chicago." This town, born with the construction of the Milwaukee Road across Montana, began in 1908 with the name of Burt. Burt became Ismay a few months later, taking its new name from Isabelle and Maybelle, daughters of railroad official George Peck. At the start of the heady settlement boom of the 1910s, Ismay had need of a deterrent for its rougher element. Bids were taken for construction of a local jail, and W. T. Perham won the contract for $676. The utilitarian brick jail of squat and sturdy construction with small windows and iron bars was built in 1910. This type of lockup was once common in rural settlements. Over the years, the building largely accommodated rowdies who overindulged at local saloons and served as a holding facility for prisoners awaiting transport to the county jail at Miles City. It is the only public building that remains from Ismay's early period. Today, the community is Montana's smallest incorporated town, and in 1993 its twenty-two residents took an unprecedented gamble. In a public relations stroke of genius that won national attention, Ismay conditionally changed its name to Joe in honor of football player Joe Montana. This entrepreneurial enterprise netted enough capital to build a new fire hall, acquire a fire truck, and restore the jail. The jail stands today as a reminder of Ismay's tenure as the "Little Chicago" of the West.

Merrill Avenue Historic District*

GLENDIVE took root as a steamboat landing on the Yellowstone River and as a railroad center in the middle of prime stock country. When the Northern Pacific Railroad reached Glendive in 1881, its first cars transported buffalo hides and bones back to the States, and river travel became a thing of the past. Soon countless head of cattle were unloaded at Glendive, filling Montana's empty prairies. Sheep and cattle ranchers enthusiastically promoted the region's grazing lands, and the town's business opportunities grew when it was designated county seat. The *Glendive Times* encouraged newcomers, even promising single women "a 'right smart' chance to catch on to husbands." By 1884, the town supported three hotels, several churches, a school, a courthouse, at least ten saloons, and a variety of other commercial enterprises. A calamitous fire in 1886 destroyed thirteen businesses, but the spirited community rebuilt in more substantial brick. A few buildings, like the Italianate-style Masonic Temple, reflect this early period. Dryland farming and homesteaders in the early 1900s had a profound impact on Glendive's economy. The 1914 neoclassical-style city hall designed by influential Miles City architect Brynulf Rivenes and the

1922 prairie-style depot, which anchor the district's opposite ends, well illustrate this prosperous era. Although railroad-related warehouses, grain elevators, and lumberyards no longer line Merrill Avenue's southeast side, this six-block district represents the years from 1886 to 1930 and tells the story of ranching, railroading, and farming in eastern Montana.

Billings Townsite Historic District*

At the turn of the twentieth century, Billings was ready to shed its frontier image as a rough-and-tumble cow town and emerge as a regional commercial center. Billings was already at the juncture of the Northern Pacific and the Chicago, Burlington, and Quincy railroads, and soon the Great Northern extended its tracks to the growing city. Platted in 1882 and named for a former railroad president, Billings became the transportation hub of the northern plains. The first business district was at the center of the townsite grid, but businesses gradually moved to the northwest as the area began catering to travelers. Between 1900 and 1920, a dozen hotels and many businesses crowded near the tracks. In 1911, a splendid depot, electric streetlights, cement sidewalks, and brick-paved streets greeted visiting President Howard Taft, who pronounced Billings "the center of the development of the arid west." Indeed, almost ten thousand homesteaders claimed land at the Billings land office between 1909 and 1914, and local hotels supported a daily transient population of at least a thousand. Billings, nicknamed Magic City for its early rapid growth, continued to mature through the 1910s. The eventual demise of rail travel left its early twentieth-century buildings vulnerable. Thanks to early preservation efforts, the district is an intact expression of turn-of-the-century commercial architecture. Its buildings, along with the depot and tracks, symbolize the town's magical beginnings and preside over what was once the heart of the townsite.

The Rattlesnake

WHEN you take the University of Montana exit off the interstate at Missoula, a right turn instead of a left will take you to the neighborhood locally known as the Rattlesnake. It's one of Missoula's best-kept secrets. Nestled in a watershed tributary of the Clark Fork River, the Lower Rattlesnake drainage has a long, significant history. Salish Indians named the creek "Stream of many salmon trout," and Captain Meriwether Lewis recorded it in 1806. William T. Hamilton operated a trading post nearby from 1858 to 1865, and the Mullan Road, built in 1860, skirted the area and crossed Rattlesnake Creek. The creek powered the Missoula Mills sawmill that provided lumber for Missoula's earliest settlement. The drainage accommodated the town's first cemetery, and the creek supplied Missoula's first water system. The Town Company and Woody Additions, platted after the Northern Pacific Railroad arrived in 1883, were home to railroad conductors and engineers as well as teamsters, carpenters, and machinists. Legislator T. L. Greenough and his wife, Tennessee, donated a large wooded area to the city in 1902 for a "comfortable, romantic and poetic retreat." Greenough Park attracted middle-income families that settled along the quiet streets. To the east, extensive gardens along the Clark Fork River provided fresh produce for the city. Today, twenty residential blocks and Greenough Park comprise the Lower Rattlesnake Historic District*. Unique for its scenic amenities and isolated geography, the district bolsters Missoula's claim as the Garden City.

Montana's National Historic Landmarks

ANCIENT brush strokes in Pictograph Cave* near Billings, glorious rustic lodges in Glacier National Park, and the log homestead of Chief Plenty Coups* west of Pryor are among several dozen extraordinary places that help define and interpret Montana's past. National Historic Landmarks illustrate our nation's history. The National Park Service administers the National Historic Landmark (NHL) program to assist federal, state, and private stewards in preserving these links to the past. Montana's NHLs interpret prehistory, Indian culture, mining, early tourism, and more. Some attract tourists from every corner of the globe, and others—every bit as spectacular—are not so well known. Seven, including the Great Falls Portage*, Three Forks of the Missouri*, Traveler's Rest* at Lolo, and Pompey's Pillar National Monument* near Billings, are pivotal to the Lewis and Clark Expedition. Sixteen miles south of Chinook along the windswept Montana High Line, hikers can follow a trail through the undeveloped landscape of the Chief Joseph Battleground of Bear's Paw National Park* and NHL. Rosebud Battlefield State Park*, east of Crow Agency near the Crow Reservation, and the Big Hole Battlefield* are NHLs that recall tragic chapters. Bannack*, Virginia City, and the Butte-Anaconda Labor Corridor* recall the importance of mining, while Fort Benton* speaks to the importance of river travel until the advent of the railroad. Grant-Kohrs National Historic Site* recalls the cattle industry. Going-to-the-Sun Road* in Glacier National Park is a feat of civil engineering. Montana's NHLs offer sweeping vistas, urban streetscapes, and ancient pathways that make a tangible connection to the past. Reach back in time and experience Montana in a journey to its National Historic Landmarks.

August Heller's Saloon*

KALISPELL already had its fair share of saloons when August Heller opened his downtown establishment in 1900. With interior fittings from Chicago, a hot water boiler, Kalispell's first cement sidewalk, and a gas lighting system, it was entirely modern. Spittoons on the floor, imported liquors, backroom poker games, and rumors of loose women upstairs kept a rough-and-tumble clientele entertained. So famous was Heller's Saloon that temperance-crusading bar smasher Carry Nation delivered her gospel message from a buggy in front of the building in 1910. Although her speech the previous evening at fifty cents a head was not particularly well attended, when citizens heard that she was to give a free speech in front of Heller's notorious saloon, a large crowd assembled. Once in front of Heller's business, Carry ranted against policemen, maintaining that they were tools of the saloons and always taking handouts from the hellholes and their agencies. Then she started in on the saloon proprietors, denouncing them as the worst men in the country except for Republicans. The Republicans, Carry exclaimed, were truly the worst. Democrats in the crowd cheered prematurely. Carry then added that conditions would be even worse if Democrats were in power. And so it went until she singled out Heller himself. But Heller got the better of her when he declared that he was an honest businessman and not a grafter like herself. Heller continued on with his lucrative career. His contributions to Kalispell's history include a whiskey bottle from his distillery found during recent renovations in a wall of the Flathead County Courthouse*.

More than Just a Home

Rockfellow House*

On a gently sloping plateau overlooking Alder Gulch, J. S. Rockfellow built the fanciest, most modern home yet constructed in Montana Territory. It was completed in time for his wedding, an affair attended by more than 150 guests in January of 1867. James Knox Polk Miller, who clerked for Rockfellow's grocery business, described the wedding, which took place at the home of W. Y. Lovell in Virginia City. Miller observed that the room was very small, the bride very little, and the ceremony very short. Carriages then conveyed the guests in their silks and finery to the mansion on the hill. The house, described in the *Montana Post*, had seven well-warmed, well-lit, and well-ventilated rooms, a luxury for sure at that time. Designed with an eye to convenience and beauty, the wallpaper and furnishings were in the best of taste. The parlor was furnished in walnut, the dining room in oak, and the bed chambers in rosewood. There were frescoed ceilings and mountain scenery in watercolors painted on the walls that, according to the reporter, spread through the house like "oriental pearls of random string." There was a system of delightfully pure spring water piped directly into the house—the first running water in Montana. The same water source fed a beautiful fountain in the yard. The house, with its tidy outbuildings perched on the hill, appeared to locals as a grand estate like no other. Unfortunately, Rockfellow died within a year, and the house on the hill fell into other hands. It still stands in Virginia City above Cover Street, an occasionally occupied eerie relic reminiscent of a tragic past.

The Castle

THERE were few settlers in the Smith River Valley when James Brewer took squatter's rights and built a cabin in 1867. The site was known for the minerals and gases that bubbled out of a thermal spring. Brewer ran a trading post until 1870 when the mining town of Diamond City moved its newspaper, doctor, and county seat to Brewer's post, giving birth to the town of White Sulphur Springs. Byron R. Sherman was among the former Diamond City residents who settled there. Sherman left a lasting imprint on White Sulphur Springs when he built his grand castle on the hill. Sherman planned it so that every window offered a sweeping view. A team of sixteen oxen hauled the granite twelve miles from the Castle Mountains to build the massive walls. Fine imported wood and delicate spindle work ornament the doors, windows, and archways. Brass and crystal light fixtures and dainty round sinks of Italian marble attest to Sherman's attention to detail. A huge wood furnace heated the castle's twelve rooms and water for the household. Pumped from a hand-dug well and powered by a windmill, the water flowed in lead pipes to the kitchen and bathrooms. Byron, his wife, Emeline, and their children moved into the house in 1893. A year later, wedding bells rang when the Shermans' son Charles was married at the castle. The next year, Emeline gave birth to a daughter, fulfilling the tradition of a wedding and a birth to make the house a home. The Shermans moved to California in the early 1900s, leaving their castle to others. Today, the Byron R. Sherman House* is a museum, open during the summer months.

Moss Mansion*

THE beautiful Moss Mansion in Billings—now a house museum—is a twenty-five-room residence built in 1903. It was the longtime home of the Preston Moss family. New York architect R. J. Hardenbergh, whose work includes New York City's Waldorf Astoria, designed the elegant mansion. Mahogany and walnut woodwork, an onyx fireplace, rose silk and gold leaf wall coverings, and stained glass windows are among the luxurious details. Preston Moss arrived in Billings in 1892 on his way to Butte from Missouri and saw Billings's financial promise. He became a prominent banker and helped develop the sugar beet industry, the Billings Light and Water Company, and the Billings Polytechnic Institute (now Rocky Mountain College). With a partner he ran eighty thousand head of sheep and several thousand head of cattle. He also pioneered the *Billings Gazette* and was instrumental in the creation of the Huntley Irrigation Project. He even started a toothpaste factory and a meat packing plant. Moss also promoted an idea he called Mossmain. This was a futuristic city he planned to build ten miles west of Billings. World War II intervened, and Preston Moss died in 1947, never realizing this dream. Melville, the Mosses' middle daughter, was seven when her family moved into the mansion. She was a talented musician and played the harp, piano, and bass from an early age. Melville traveled the world and never married, but the mansion was her home throughout her life. She died in 1984 at eighty-two. Because of Melville's good stewardship, the grand interiors remain unchanged today.

Original Governor's Mansion*

IN 1913, the Montana State Legislature appropriated thirty thousand dollars to purchase the former Chessman Mansion for use as the executive residence. Previous governors had supplied their own housing. The state selected the Chessman house because it was close to the Capitol and elegant and roomy enough for small state functions. Governor Samuel Stewart was the first governor in residence. He and his wife, Stella, their three small daughters, Emily, Marjorie, and Leah, and Stella's parents, along with service staff, made a large household. The state's purchase included the elaborate table and chairs that still grace the dining room. Ornately carved men hold the table on their shoulders, and animal heads with open mouths top the chair frames. Emily recalled those open mouths "made wonderful places to park a wad of gum." The bathroom was one of Helena's first as Mr. Chessman developed the early water system. Leah had one unpleasant memory of that bathroom, whose original fixtures were still in use by the Stewart family. During a drought in 1917 or 1918, as Stella drew a bath for Leah in the footed tub, a worm came out of the tap. Leah never wanted to take a bath after that. As the governor's executive mansion, the first floor was public space for state functions and entertaining. The upper two floors were very much the family home. Stella Stewart was a loving mother, and the daughters recalled with nostalgia that she would put Schubert's serenade "Leise flehen meine Lieder" on the victrola in the upstairs sitting room. As the music filtered through the upstairs rooms, the girls knew it was time for bed.

Conrad Mansion*

ALICIA "LETTIE" CONRAD never let adversity get the better of her. When her Kalispell mansion almost burned down in October 1910, the entire town turned out to fight the blaze. The house survived, and before it was repaired, she used the scorched walls and wet furniture as a set for a spectacular Halloween party. She invited all of Kalispell in gratitude. But when Lettie died in 1923, her beloved mansion fell into decay. The City of Kalispell acquired the property, and many gave money and time to restore it. In the 1980s,

Arvid "Kris" Kristoffersen did the interior painting. While working on this project, he experienced two eerie events. One afternoon, Kris was alone in a second-floor bedroom when he heard female footsteps coming down the hallway. He looked up to see a slightly heavyset woman in a white, ankle-length dress. Kris went to the doorway and watched the figure disappear down the stairs. Her footsteps faded into the kitchen. A few days later, Kris and his partner were working downstairs alone in the quiet house. A noise at the top of the stairs caught their attention. Looking up, they both saw an empty rocking chair moving back and forth, creaking. The two men gathered their paintbrushes and called it a day. Kris felt sure that Lettie paid them a visit to check on their work. Some months later, museum employees were sorting through clothing left in an upstairs closet. They found a very old, ankle-length white dress. Kris identified it as the same dress worn by the ghostly woman in the hallway.

Daly Mansion*

With Marcus Daly's death in 1900, Margaret Daly stopped plans to build a new residence in the Bitterroot Valley. In 1906, Margaret decided to go ahead with her plans and commissioned prominent Missoula architect A. J. Gibson to design a new mansion that would replace the Dalys' outdated Queen Anne–style home. Completed in 1910, it served as Margaret Daly's summer residence until her death at the mansion in 1941. Marcus Daly began buying Bitterroot Valley land in 1887 and eventually owned twenty-eight thousand acres, where he raised fine thoroughbred racehorses on his Bitter Root Stock Farm. After Daly's death, Mrs. Daly managed local family properties and the family syndicate that oversaw Daly interests. She loved the Bitterroot Valley and held court like royalty. The Georgian revival mansion was the most lavish, largest summer home anywhere in the West. There were twenty-four bedrooms, fifteen bathrooms, and three dining rooms. Seven

Italian marble fireplaces, door knobs in cut glass and brass, thirteen bells to summon servants, and bathtubs edged in gold reflect the Dalys' sumptuous lifestyle at Riverside. Because the Panic of 1893 destroyed many mining-based fortunes in Montana and out-of-state investors financed later mining ventures, copper kings no longer lived in Montana, and grand homes were a thing of the past by the time Mrs. Daly constructed Riverside. The home's outstanding features, elegant and regal yet understated, much like Mrs. Daly herself, include a monumental classical portico, symmetrical façade, and roof deck edged in balusters. In 1987, the heirs donated the mansion in exchange for forgiveness of a portion of taxes, and it is maintained as a house museum. The interior finishing, furnishings, and professionally landscaped grounds remain unchanged from 1910.

Greenough Mansion*

Missoula's Greenough Mansion tragically went up in flames in 1992. At the time, hundreds of locals passed by the ruins, paying homage to golden memories of weddings, anniversaries, and special occasions celebrated in the once-beautiful Victorian home. Thomas Greenough made a fortune in the lumber business and spent a good portion of it on the home he built for his wife, Tennessee. Designed by A. J. Gibson in the mid-1890s, the mansion nestled at the end of Vine Street along the banks of Rattlesnake Creek. It had ten bedrooms, a grand ballroom, hand-painted wallpaper, and woodwork cut from tamarack trees in the Rattlesnake Valley. Tennessee raised the couple's six children in the mansion, mostly while her husband traveled making money. After his death in 1911, the house became a choice location for weddings and other special events. The construction of Interstate 90 almost spelled its demise. But son-in-law A. J. Mosby, who pioneered Missoula's first television and radio stations, determined to move it to out of

Stan Healy, photographer, Archives and Special Collections, Mansfield Library, University of Montana, Missoula, 90.1634

Missoula's Greenough Mansion awaits the move across town to make way for Interstate 90 in 1965.

the path of progress to his golf course on the south side of town. The house got as far as Van Buren Street and encountered a major setback. None of the existing bridges across the Clark Fork could bear its 287 tons. It sat for sixteen months and suffered deterioration and interior damage from a fire. Finally, the house was partially disassembled, cut into three pieces, moved to its new location, and put back together. Many of its original details were carefully preserved, including the pull-chain flush on the commode in the ladies' lounge. The mansion perched atop the hillside in its new setting for another quarter century before it finally succumbed to fire.

Copper King Mansion*

BUTTE'S Copper King Mansion commands a sprawling view of the city that spreads around it. Self-made multimillionaire William Clark spent an estimated $260,000 on the construction of his incredible thirty-two-room residence, built between 1884 and 1888. Though an astounding sum back then, that figure represented only a half-day's worth of Clark's earnings. Clark's monthly income was $17 million. Building this Queen Anne–style mansion would have been an accomplishment in the most cosmopolitan cities, but in remote 1880s Butte, Montana, it was an astounding feat. Porticos, arches, and elaborate exterior ornamentation only hint at the opulence inside. Each room features a different kind of wood and a unique hand-painted ceiling. There are Tiffany stained glass windows and chandeliers and an intricately carved staircase. Clark spared no expense, equipping his home with all the amenities and the latest technology the 1880s had to offer, including three types of lighting: electric, incandescent, and gas. There was a complete system of electric call bells, and a 1,500-gallon tank on the third floor supplied the household with running water. A French shower, called a needle bath, is still functional in one of the bathrooms. In the basement, boilers provided indirect heating to the first and second floors while radiators heated the third story. Windows of beveled French plate glass have blinds of hardwood that fold into pockets. The home is exactly as it was in the 1880s, with the original 1884 paint undisturbed on the walls. Today, the mansion is a bed-and-breakfast where you can truly wrap yourself in the past and even experience Clark's fully functional needle bath.

T. Byron Story Mansion*

 ARCHITECT C. S. Haire, renowned for his design of the wings on the Montana State Capitol, designed this Bozeman home

28

in 1910 for the wealthy Thomas Byron Story family. Story was a son of Nelson Story, the pioneer entrepreneur who brought the first Texas longhorns into Montana Territory in 1866 and amassed a fortune in the cattle industry. T. Byron and his wife, Katherine, had five children and wanted room for their boisterous family. Haire drew his plans from various architectural styles, including Queen Anne, shingle, and Tudor revival. The mansion's steeply pitched roofs, inviting porch, semicircular tower, and covered carriage entrance create a distinctive silhouette. Diverse building materials add visual interest: stone from Bridger Canyon lines the foundation, and brick from Hebron, North Dakota, defines the first story. Shingles and false half-timbering decorate the upper stories. One of three Montana mansions occupying an entire block, the nine-thousand-square-foot, twenty-two-room home cost an estimated fifty thousand dollars to build, more than ten times the average Bozeman residence of the early 1900s. T. Byron's wealth came from management of extensive family holdings. He amassed his own fortune during World War I by supplying wool for military uniforms and milling Montana wheat. Financial setbacks during the depressed later 1910s and 1920s forced T. Byron to sell the property in 1922 to the Sigma Alpha Epsilon fraternity. The fraternity owned the property until 2003 when the City of Bozeman purchased the home. It remains in public ownership.

Rest in Peace

John Colter's Ghost

JOHN COLTER and John Potts of the Lewis and Clark Expedition returned to the Three Forks area in 1808 to trap. They were in dangerous Blackfeet country, so they hid by day and trapped by night. But one day Blackfeet surprised them and killed Potts. They stripped Colter and told him to run. He ran so hard that blood ran from his mouth and nose onto his chest, but he did survive to tell the story. Some forty years later in 1849, Jim Baker—who later wrote of this incident—was guiding a party of trappers in the area. One of the men was a brave but superstitious trapper named Bertram Emanuel. One night as Emanuel sat with his back against a tree on watch, the full moon lit up the landscape, and he could see for some distance. Suddenly a figure arose from nowhere and came toward the camp. Emanuel could see that he was naked, and he moved toward the riverbank in a peculiar way. Emanuel approached the man with his gun ready. The figure whirled to face him and threw his arms over his head. Blood was streaming from his nose and mouth, covering his chest. The figure ran to the riverbank and disappeared into thin air. Emanuel was greatly disturbed and related his experience in detail the next morning. Two members of the group agreed that their camp was on the spot where Potts had

30

been killed and Colter forced to run. Colter's ghost was warning them. They hurriedly packed and left the place. It was a good thing because they barely missed the Blackfeet traveling up the river.

First Missoula Cemetery

In the summer of 1974, a Missoula homeowner was adding a porch to his house on Cherry Street when he got a big surprise. The backhoe digging the foundation unearthed something that should not have been there: human bones. The coroner confirmed the discovery of two sets of bones encased in the decayed wood of old-fashioned coffins. Authorities determined that no foul play was involved. These were simply historic burials, the individuals placed in the ground by loved ones hoping for their eternal rest. The pieces of metal hardware, splintered wood, and bone fragments were collected in a box that today sits on a shelf in a University of Montana laboratory. The bones serve as teaching tools for anthropology students. Those who have studied the contents of the box have solved some of the mystery. Historic maps of Missoula and newspaper clippings show that Missoula's first cemetery was located in the area in 1865. It fell into disuse with the opening of the current city cemetery in 1884, and the last burial there occurred in 1895. When the land was subdivided in the 1940s, traces of the old cemetery disappeared, but, according to city records, most burials were not removed. This is not particularly uncommon. Other Montana communities have subdivisions located on historic burial grounds. Helena's Robinson Park and its adjacent residential streets, built over the town's first Catholic cemetery, is one example. But to whom did the two sets of bones belong? Students determined long ago that one was a child and the other a female adult. Coffin hardware fragments were consistent with nineteenth-century casket styles. But whose eternal sleep was so rudely interrupted? That is a part of the mystery that will probably never be solved.

George Drouillard's Luck Runs Out

GEORGE DROUILLARD was an interpreter and hunter for the Lewis and Clark Corps of Discovery. He was half Shawnee Indian and half French Canadian, and both captains praised him as essential for the subsistence of the men. He had tremendous skills as a hunter and woodsman and an uncommon knowledge of sign language. The captains wrote that he handled the most dangerous and trying adventures with the greatest of courage. Like other members of the Lewis and Clark Expedition, Drouillard returned to the area that would become Montana with fur trading and trapping expeditions. He explored the Big Horn drainage and mountains, adding his knowledge to William Clark's evolving map of the West. In May of 1810, although fearful of Indian attacks, Drouillard was among twenty-one men of the Missouri Fur Company who left their fort at the Missouri headwaters and made camp up the Jefferson River to trap beaver. Drouillard confidently went out from that camp twice, although cautioned not to travel alone, and trapped with success. But on the third day, his luck ran out. Indians attacked him and two others who had followed him, hacking them to pieces. The trapper who discovered the gruesome scene later wrote: "Druyer and his horse lay dead . . . he must have fought in a circle on horseback and probably killed some of his enemies, being a brave man and well armed with a rifle, pistol, knife and tomahawk." George Droulliard died in the Three Forks vicinity and is buried in an unmarked grave where a fishing access is named for him.

Place Where the White Horse Went Down

A SMALLPOX epidemic in 1837–38 caused widespread devastation among Montana's native people. The disease spread from the American Fur Trading Company's steamboat *St. Peters* as it lay docked laden with trade goods at Fort Union. The steamboat captain refused to quarantine the passengers and crew, fearing repercussions if trade goods were not distributed. While tribes below Fort Pierre in present-day South Dakota had been vaccinated against the disease in 1832, most of Montana's tribes were unexposed to the disease and unprotected. Some estimate that ten thousand Blackfeet died during this epidemic. It wiped out 94 percent of the Assiniboines and hundreds of Crows. Historian and storyteller Joe Medicine Crow tells a terrible story about this epidemic. Two young Crow warriors returning from a war expedition found their village stricken with the sickness. One discovered his sweetheart among the dead and dying. Both warriors, grieving over the loss of their entire families and many friends, were inconsolable, despondent, and frustrated because nothing could alter the terrible course of events. The young warriors dressed in their finest clothing and mounted a snow white horse. Riding double and singing their death songs, they drove the blindfolded horse over a cliff and landed at what is now the eastern end of the Yellowstone County Fairgrounds. Teenage witnesses to the drama buried the dead warriors where they fell. Great loss of life among the Crows followed in the wake of the epidemic. Although time has reduced the height of the cliff, the location is remembered even today as the Place Where the White Horse Went Down. A highway marker commemorates the site of this event.

Brother Van's Love Story

MONTANA's famous itinerant Methodist minister, William Wesley Van Orsdel, known to most as "Brother Van," never married but was once engaged. As Brother Van traveled across Montana Territory in the 1870s, he stopped at the sheep ranch of Richard Reynolds in the Beaverhead Valley. The family invited him to stay, and there he met Reynolds's stepdaughter, thirteen-year-old Jennie Johnston. She and Brother Van became fast friends. When Jennie turned eighteen, Brother Van was thirty-one. Jennie's mother wanted her to go to college, and so in September 1879, she and Brother Van postponed their plans to marry while Jennie attended Northwest University in Evanston, Illinois. Jennie soon became ill with tuberculosis. In summer 1880, she returned home to Montana. The next February, Jennie caught the measles but recovered and helped nurse other family members through what was then a very dangerous illness. But by summer 1881, Jennie's health began to fail. She died in October. As she lay in her casket in the Reynolds' parlor, Brother Van slipped the wedding ring he would have given her onto her finger. He wore the ring she would have given him for the rest of his life. Jennie, whose mother was a Poindexter, was buried in the Poindexter family cemetery that today is in a cow pasture. Jennie's grave was moved to Mountain View Cemetery northeast of Dillon and is marked with only a small nameplate. Brother Van lived a long, full life and died in 1919. He is buried in Helena, far from his beloved Jennie.

William "Brother Van" Van Orsdel (left, with hand inside his coat) at the wedding of Helena newsman Charles Greenfield and Elizabeth Nelson in 1913, probably at her Vandalia home near Glasgow

Montana Historical Society Photograph Archives, Helena, 942.477

Isaiah Dorman, "Black White Man"

ALTHOUGH no African American buffalo soldiers fought in the Battle of the Little Big Horn, there was one black interpreter who fell with Custer. There is much conflicting information about Isaiah Dorman. One source claims that he was born free, another that he was a slave, and still others claim that nothing is known of his background except that he spent much of his adult life on the plains involved in trading on the Missouri River. Dorman lived with the Sioux and spoke the Lakota language fluently. The army hired him as a courier in 1865 to carry the payroll, and in 1871 he served as the guide and escort for Northern Pacific Railroad surveyors as they scouted the route the railroad would later take through Montana. He accompanied the explorers on the early Yellowstone expeditions. Dorman also served as post interpreter at Fort Rice, North Dakota. General George Custer requested his services as U.S. Army interpreter. Dorman was married to a Lakota woman and did not want to accompany Custer to the Little Big Horn, but Custer persuaded him, offering a pay raise from fifty to seventy-five dollars a month. He was never paid. A Sioux warrior found Dorman dying on the battlefield, severely wounded, his legs riddled with bullets. He reportedly said to his companions, "This is the black white man. He used to be one of us." Dorman was the only African American known to die in the Battle of the Little Big Horn, ironically working for those fighting against the people who had taken him in.

Nancy Wright's Sacrifice

EIGHT miles above Alder Gulch, along a narrow and winding wagon road that leads to the ghost town of Summit, a lonely grave keeps vigil. Four sturdy pine trees, one at each corner of the small burial plot, mark the final resting place of Nancy Millsop Wright. Readily visible from the treacherous road where heavily

35

laden oxen and mule teams labored, this grave speaks to the heartache and hardship of many early Montana pioneers. Nancy Wright came to Summit around 1865 with her two small sons, John and Frank, to join her husband, William. He was a millwright who built and operated a stamp mill along Spring Creek. The family made their home where William operated his mill. Nancy bore three more children while the family lived at Summit: George in 1866, Alpharetta in 1867, and Harry in January of 1869. At Harry's birth, however, Nancy's health failed. She realized that she had not long to live and that she could not be buried in the cemetery at Virginia City. It was a severe winter, and passage down the mountain was impossible because of heavy snow. So she chose a place near her home. In a story all too common on the frontier, the Wright family scattered when the mill closed and William could not care for his children. A Sheridan family adopted newborn Harry, the Switzer family took in Alpharetta, the two younger boys found homes in the Madison Valley, and the oldest son, John, stayed with his father, who moved on. An empty bottle lies today on Nancy Wright's remote grave, where visitors sometimes place a prayer or a message in observance of her poignant sacrifice.

Jack Slade's Funeral

HISTORIANS will never stop bickering about whether or not vigilante hangings were justified. Most historians would agree, however, that Jack Slade's execution was unwarranted. Slade was a public menace, but he did nothing more than disturb the peace. His hanging, however, was one of Montana's most dramatic events. Slade's wife, Virginia, rode screaming into town on her black stallion Billy Bay. She was only seconds too late. Mary Ronan, a child of ten at the time, years later told her daughter, "My heart ached for Mrs. Slade. I slipped away from home, determined to tell her how sorry I was. I found her sobbing and moaning over a stark form shrouded in a blanket. I stood beside her trembling and choking, then I slipped away unnoticed." Harriet Sanders loaned Virginia a pair of black stockings for the funeral and attended the service more out of curiosity than sorrow for the fate of Jack Slade. She mostly wondered what the minister would say about him. The preacher began by explaining, "It has always been my practice when preaching funeral sermons to make little or no reference to the dead, and I will not digress from my usual habit." And he never mentioned Slade throughout the entire service. Virginia Slade refused to bury her husband in Virginia City. Legend says she had Jack's body sealed in a zinc-lined coffin filled with the whiskey that was his undoing. Contrary to popular belief, she did not keep him in town, but took his casket to her home in the Meadow Valley along the Bozeman Road north of town where she and her husband had collected tolls from travelers. When the snow melted, she took him to Salt Lake City for proper burial.

Lloyd Magruder's Grisly End

THE vast Territory of Idaho, created in 1863, included the western half of Montana and had its capital at Lewiston, Idaho. Hill Beachy ran a hotel and stage stop at Lewiston. One night he dreamed that his good friend Lloyd Magruder, an Elk City, Idaho, merchant, was returning from Virginia City with a fortune in gold dust. According to Beachy's dream, as Magruder and his companions camped west of Nez Perce Pass, thieves ambushed and killed them. This nightmare horrified Beachy, but his wife cautioned him not to talk about it or people would think he was crazy. Meanwhile, Lloyd Magruder set off for Virginia City with a load of goods to sell. When he did not return at the appointed time, Beachy feared his dream had come true. Soon after, a group of four men came into Lewiston behaving in a suspicious manner. Beachy suspected these men had killed his friend. They bought tickets on the stage and left some items at the local livery. A youngster who had worked for Magruder recognized his horse and saddle. Beachy persuaded the judge to issue a warrant, and he hunted down the desperadoes. They stood trial, and three of them were hung. These were the first legal hangings in Idaho Territory. Hill Beachy later visited the site where Magruder and his four companions were killed. Their bodies had been wrapped in blankets and thrown over a cliff. Beachy recovered the remains and buried them. The remote route the ill-fated merchant took across the Continental Divide to Elk City is known today as Magruder's Corridor.

Paul Maclean's Unsolved Murder

NORMAN MACLEAN's novella, *A River Runs Through It*, has an interesting back story. As youngsters, Norman and his brother Paul lived in Helena and Missoula, where their father was a Presbyterian minister. The brothers were fighters and daredevils, and some still remember their antics. Paul later worked for the Helena and Great Falls newspapers, earning a fine reputation as House reporter during the 1930s legislative sessions. In 1938, Norman was teaching at the University of Chicago, and Paul had almost completed his master's degree in English there. In the wee hours of May 3, 1938, Paul was beaten to death in a back alley. Terry Dwyer of the *Great Falls Tribune* worked with Paul and knew him as a good reporter, but also as a man who would never back down from a fight. Many believed Paul's murder was mob related—that he owed money, or knew something for which he needed silencing. But the murder was never solved, and Norman had to come to terms with his brother's death. After he retired from teaching Shakespeare, Norman, at the age of seventy, took up writing. He cast his wild brother as that artistically perfect, but flawed, fly fisherman in *A River Runs Through It*. As Norman wrote the novella so many years later, he confronted demons of the past, discussing his brother's death publicly for the first time. Norman's daughter, Jean Maclean Snyder, told the *Livingston Enterprise* that her father believed you come to terms with something by understanding it. Norman finally reconciled Paul's senseless death through his writing. "All good things," he wrote, "come by grace and grace comes by art and art does not come easy."

Coulson

ON a hill overlooking modern-day Billings, Boothill Cemetery* recalls the roots of an earlier, short-lived community called Coulson. In 1877, founders named the little town after the Coulson Packet Line, a steamboat company that operated on the Missouri River above Sioux City, Dakota Territory. The theory was that if they built the town on the Yellowstone River, steamboats would come. The Yellowstone Valley was soon full of settlers, and Coulson was an up-and-coming town, a product of the wildest west. It boasted many saloons, but it had neither church nor school, and few steamboats made it up the river that far. Residents believed that Coulson would be a shipping point for livestock when the Northern Pacific Railroad arrived, but the railroad chose a different location. Railroad officials located their new townsite two miles away on an alkali flat in 1883. They named it after Frederick Billings, past president of the Northern Pacific. Coulson moved its tents and buildings to the new town, and nothing—not even foundations—remains to remind visitors of that early community. Coulson left behind only its dead. Some thirty-five souls rest on the hill overlooking modern Billings, buried there from 1877 to 1882. They were victims of typhoid, accidents, suicide, and murder. Boothill Cemetery is a landmark that recalls the first local settlement. In 1982, the Yellowstone Historical Society commemorated the centennial of Coulson's demise, marking this last remnant with a plaque. It reads: "Coulson 1877–1882. Born by the River and killed by the Railroad, giving to Billings her best citizens, to Boothill her residue, to the Yellowstone her memories."

Lynching of Frank Little

In June 1917, a strike broke out in the aftermath of the deadly Speculator Mine disaster where more than 160 miners lost their lives. Frank Little, one of the "toughest, most courageous and impulsive" leaders of the Industrial Workers of the World, or IWW, came to Butte to support the strike and draw miners into the organization. The IWW was an industrial union committed to the overthrow of the capitalist system by a working-class revolution. Many Butte miners supported Little's speeches against the Anaconda Company, the draft, and World War I, but company executives and others feared his words. Although the company and local officials pushed for Little's arrest for "treasonable utterances," U.S. district attorney Burton K. Wheeler found insufficient evidence to indict him. In the early morning of August 1, six masked vigilantes entered the boardinghouse where Little was living. They forced him, still in his underwear, to the waiting car outside. A short distance away, they tied Little to the back of the car and dragged him to the outskirts of town. The men beat him to death and hung his body from a railroad trestle. Pinned to the corpse was the old vigilante warning, 3-7-77. An estimated 6,800 people marched in Little's funeral procession, the largest in Butte's history. His tombstone in Mountain View Cemetery reads, "Slain by the capitalist interests for organizing and inspiring his fellow men." No one was ever charged with the crime.

Frenchtown

Even before the Mullan Road from Walla Walla to Fort Benton—built between 1859 and 1860—reached the Missoula Valley, French-Canadian Catholics settled at Frenchtown to farm. By 1859, these early settlers operated a mill. Many men who worked on the labor crews building the Mullan Road returned to the area to settle. Among them were Louis Brun, who operated the first roadhouse along the Mullan Road, and Moses Reeves, who had the contract to carry the mail from Walla Walla to Fort Benton. In 1864, Jesuit priests from St. Ignatius Mission* established the Frenchtown Cemetery and built a small log church, the second in Montana for white settlers. They named it the St. Louis Church after the pious French king whom Jesuits believed a worthy role model. The church no longer stands, but the historic cemetery is Frenchtown's most significant site. The stone monuments, many with French names, point to the ethnic origins of these earliest families. A high wrought-iron fence, family plots, and handsome stones make it one of Montana's most charming cemeteries. Among the tombstones are those of Frenchtown's founding families. The stone mausoleum of T. J. De Mers, wealthy founder of the Flathead Valley boomtown of Demersville, holds his remains and those of eleven family members. The 264 recorded burials include worn wooden markers and elaborate marble tombstones. That of Moses Reeves's wife Josette, dated 1873, is the cemetery's oldest marked grave, but there are many unmarked graves from the earliest time period. The cemetery remains an active burial ground for descendants of Frenchtown's founding families.

Cemetery Island

THE last remaining symbol of the once-bustling community of Canyon Ferry today lies on an island rising high above the deep waters of this popular recreation spot. But once this lonely cemetery served a vibrant community. Established in 1865, the mining camp and supply center at Canyon Ferry, where there was a convenient Missouri River crossing, was home to some of the earliest local pioneer families. Although the oldest recorded grave dates to 1874, local lore insists that the cemetery includes many unmarked graves dating from the 1860s. A number of them, originally marked with wooden slabs long since weathered away, were the final resting places of victims of the infamous claim-jumper war at nearby Cave Gulch. Old-timers remembered that whenever there was a burial, mourners walked up the hill, following behind the horse-drawn wagon that served as a hearse. At the top of the rise, funeral services commended the loved one to the earth. But by the 1940s, the historic cemetery sat in a horse pasture surrounded by a sea of gently rolling fields. In the late 1940s, plans for the Canyon Ferry Dam put the cemetery in jeopardy. The Bureau of Reclamation offered families a choice: leave the graves in place or move them elsewhere. There are no records documenting relocations by families, although the *Independent Record* noted in 1949 that unmarked graves were moved to the cemetery near Winston. In 1952, the area was flooded, creating Canyon Ferry Lake. Today, sparkling blue water, not gently rolling fields, surrounds what is known as Cemetery Island.

Conrad Cemetery

THE Conrad Memorial Cemetery in Kalispell is one of Montana's most beautiful places. Sited on a promontory overlooking the entire Flathead Valley, it is an especially lovely and peaceful location for a final resting place. Just before town father Charles Conrad died in 1902, he told his wife, Alicia, that he wanted to be buried on the promontory near the family home, where the land steeply sloped to the Whitefish River. On this spot he and Alicia had taken their last horseback ride together and experienced the sweeping beauty of that very special place. Conrad instructed his attorney to purchase the land and the ten acres surrounding it. The attorney carried out his instructions, and Mrs. Conrad and her daughter began touring cemeteries in the United States, Canada, and Mexico for design ideas. On their travels they met A. W. Hobert, a Minneapolis landscape architect. They invited him to Kalispell to survey the location of the proposed cemetery. When he visited the site, he told Mrs. Conrad, "I cannot improve upon God's architecture. My advice is to disturb as little as possible. Do not remove a shovelful of earth that is not necessary. You already have one of the most beautiful cemetery sites in the world." Mrs. Conrad commissioned Hobert to design the cemetery. Unlike standard churchyard or pioneer burial grounds, the Conrad Cemetery draws upon rural garden and French Parisian cemetery concepts, using the natural flow of the land. The Conrad cemetery association formed in 1905. Since that time, there have been more than 17,850 burials. The Conrads would be pleased to know that their vision remains almost unchanged.

Demise of the York Block

On the morning of September 17, 1898, at about 10:30, a miraculous event occurred on Butte's West Park Street where the Phoenix Building* stands today. The ground floor of the York Block was under renovation. Support posts had been removed and temporary framework substituted. There were fourteen workmen on the ground floor and half a dozen lodgers in the upstairs rooming house. Suddenly the entire building quivered, and then there were ominous cracking sounds. The workmen dashed out as the whole front half of the building collapsed into the basement. Some of the men were caught under falling debris, but they crawled out with only cuts and bruises. The boardinghouse keeper fell from the second floor to the basement, breaking her shoulder. Her daughter jumped from a third-floor window onto the roof next door and was uninjured. Two other female residents also safely jumped onto a neighboring roof. The entire front of the building to within twenty feet of the rear disappeared. The collapse sent such a rush of air that it blew a gentleman lodger on the second floor to the undisturbed back portion of the building. Another lodger, a police officer, was getting ready for work. He suddenly found himself teetering on the very edge of the wreck, with only a swirl of thick dust where his room had been seconds before. The fire department and citizens furiously removed debris, freeing all those trapped. The boarding-house keeper's broken shoulder was the most serious injury. Had the accident happened at night when the lodgers were at home and in bed, fifty people would have gone down in the wreck. Buried beneath the Phoenix Block lie the ruins of the York. May they rest in peace.

Legal and Illegal Capers

Capital Shenanigans

SETH BULLOCK of Deadwood fame represented Lewis and Clark County in the early territorial legislature in Virginia City. Bullock and legislators Granville Stuart and R. O. Hickman were desperate to find living quarters during the long session as all the hotel rooms were full. The three found a room above a saloon in a crude frame building. The wind whistled through gaps in the walls. A stove sat in the middle of the room, and all three shared the one large bed, keeping each other warm as temperatures dipped below zero. The room was a popular gathering place for legislators. Wilbur Sanders and others were visiting one evening while Baron O'Keefe was in town lobbying the legislature for money to build a bridge across the Hell Gate River. He refused to pay the toll on the existing bridge and was tired of swimming his horse across with his clothes in his arms. On this evening O'Keefe sat below in the saloon, dozing by the stove after a few stiff drinks. Upstairs, Sanders got up to get a drink of water, complaining there was nothing stronger. The dipper had frozen in the rim of ice on the top of the bucket. In prying it loose, the bucket overturned and icy water spilled through the floor onto Baron O'Keefe. He jolted awake, grabbed his Colt revolver, and fired three shots into the ceiling. The bartender knew who was visiting upstairs. He grabbed the gun before O'Keefe could fire again.

45

They scrambled upstairs to find no harm done. The Baron invited them downstairs and bought them drinks. "To think," he said, "I might have killed someone that's voting for my bridge!"

Capitol Commissions

THE Montana State Capitol* had a colorful and controversial history even before it was built. The first Capitol Commission, appointed in the 1890s and charged with the building's construction, was accused of inflating costs and pocketing the excess. The grand jury identified state architect John C. Paulsen as its key witness. But the investigation was put to rest only when Paulsen committed suicide the evening before his testimony. To convict members of the commission, Paulsen would have had to incriminate himself for participating in similar schemes on other state building projects. Governor Robert B. Smith appointed a new commission, and that group chose architects J. H. Kent and C. E. Bell to design the building. Even that was not without controversy. The Capitol's most conspicuous element, the copper-clad dome, received much scrutiny. Kent's original plans called for a more economical, unremarkable dome with a gentle slope and flat top. The Capitol Commission decided that Kent's design was embarrassingly frugal. Bell agreed. As planning time ran out in 1901, engineers increased the area of the dome by ninety feet. A push-up center and sloping sides allowed greater height with minimal structural change, and of course, the dome was to be clad in native Montana copper. While others praised the beautiful finished dome, its architect unhappily wrote: "I made *my* design . . . dignified and reposeful, but the Commission, backed by my partner, induced me to raise the Crown of the dome, and so it remains the only really imperfect feature (tho alas the most prominent one) of an otherwise pretty good looking building."

Seventh Legislative Session

As the year 1900 drew to a close, Helena prepared for Montana's seventh legislative session. The Capitol was under construction and not ready for occupancy, so the state arranged to hold the session at the Merchants Hotel on Broadway. It would be the fourth session held at the Merchants. Previous sessions had been held at various places, including the Electric Block, the Power Block*, and the courthouse, but the two houses had met under one roof for the first time at the Merchants Hotel in 1895. The old hotel had been closed since the 1899 session. It was too expensive to run and could not compete with the Queen City's two newer hostelries, the Grandon and the Helena. The state agreed to provide its own heat and rented the building for five hundred dollars. Dusting off the cobwebs, the Senate and the House would meet on the first floor with the committee rooms on the second floor. When a joint session was necessary, legislators would simply move to the public auditorium, which sat at Warren and Seventh next to Central School*. There was a rumor that temperance leaders had complained to the governor, asking that the saloon in the hotel's basement not be open for business during the session as it had been in the past. It's not known how the governor handled the complaint, but this was the last legislative session where open bars on the premises were discussed. The new Capitol was open for the next session in 1903, and open bars on-site were no longer an issue.

Seth Bullock and the First Legal Hanging

SETH BULLOCK, featured in the popular series *Deadwood*, was a real person who was prominent in Montana before he became sheriff at Deadwood, South Dakota. There is no record of the hanging of Clell Watson at Helena, depicted in the series' first episode. The event seems to have no basis in fact. However, Bullock did serve in the Montana territorial legislature, was elected sheriff of Lewis and Clark County in 1873, and presided over the first legal hanging conducted in the Territory of Montana. William Wheatley was sentenced to hang for the brutal murder of Franz Warl. The judge set the execution for Friday, August 13, 1875. By law the sheriff had to invite a physician, a county attorney, twelve citizen witnesses, his staff, the presiding judge, officers of the court, and members of the press. Sheriffs sometimes sent more than one hundred invitations, and large crowds attended these legal executions. Sheriff Bullock constructed a scaffold for the hanging in the jail yard behind the Lewis and Clark County Courthouse in Helena but then realized that the height of the scaffold would allow many more witnesses than those invited. The law prohibited the public from witnessing executions. So Sheriff Bullock built as tall a fence as he could around the scaffold. There were, however, many buildings around the courthouse with roofs convenient for spectators, and Bullock realized he could not prevent the public from witnessing the hanging. So he changed the scheduled time of the hanging to midnight. Even so, at the appointed time so many climbed the roofs that they were in danger of collapse, and more than a thousand people witnessed Wheatley's orderly hanging by the light of the moon.

Gallows Barn

On October 6, 1916, seven black railroad workers boarded a freight train at Nihill in Wheatland County. As the train got under way, all seven pulled out weapons, robbed the three white passengers in the car, and shot all three victims. One victim, Michael Freeman, died. Authorities arrested all seven men. Three of the seven—Henry Hall, Leslie Fahley, and Harrison Gibson—received the death penalty for Freeman's murder. The case was highly controversial because advocates claimed race played a role in the verdict and that because the three black men were illiterate, they could neither understand the court proceedings nor their rights. Some advocated executive clemency, but Governor Sam Stewart, who was a strong proponent of capital punishment, refused to commute the sentences. The governor concluded the trial was fair and that the crime recalled the days when gangs of road agents preyed upon travelers. The similar circumstances demanded like punishment. The triple hanging took place at White Sulphur Springs in Meagher County on February 16, 1917. There had been no legal hanging in Montana since 1909, and so there was no working gallows available. With pieces of an 1884 scaffold, officials constructed a gallows inside a cavernous county-owned barn. There was further public outcry because the barn sat a hundred yards from the public school, and the hangings were to take place during the morning when school was in session. However, the three simultaneous executions took place as scheduled. Among the forty witnesses was one of the three robbery victims. In 1975, the barn with its gallows intact was removed to Nevada City, Montana, where it is still on display.

First Female at Deer Lodge

TWENTY-one-year-old Felicita Sanchez was a newcomer to Missoula in 1878. Those who frequented the seamy side of the bustling frontier town of Deer Lodge knew her to be adept with a pistol and knife. She arrived at Missoula intent upon opening a lower-class bordello and found a vacant house on the outskirts of town. Tom Kelley, a well-known drunkard with a bad temper, had spread his blankets in the front room. Felicita asked him to move out. As Kelley gathered his things, she drew a pistol and shot him three times, instantly snuffing out his life. She never explained her motive. Deputy Sheriff Thomas Andrews escorted Felicita to the Montana Territorial Prison* at Deer Lodge to begin a three-year sentence for manslaughter. She was the prison's first female inmate.

Deputy Andrews ushered her into an office, where she promptly put both feet up on the stove, rolled a cigarette, and smoked it with relish. The warden, already uncomfortable with her unladylike behavior, took half an hour to fill out the required receipt. The next step was to discover if the convict had any weapons or contraband on her person. Deputy Andrews declined to search her, and showed Felicita to her cell. The newspaper reported that three guards resigned, refusing to guard a woman prisoner. A fourth guard agreed to stay on the condition that Felicita be held in a cell especially well fortified. There were no matrons or female attendants in the territorial prison. The men charged with guarding Felicita breathed a collective sigh of relief when territorial governor Benjamin Potts signed her early release in 1880 after she had served a little more than half her sentence.

Bessie Fisher

FEW women in early twentieth-century Montana served time at the Montana State Prison in Deer Lodge. Bessie Fisher, a diminutive nineteen-year-old black prostitute from Butte, was an exception. The court's severe punishment in 1901 suggests that Bessie's race, her occupation, and the all-male court condemned her before she was tried. Bessie, an admitted morphine addict, stood accused of the second-degree murder of "Big Eva" Frye. She feared she would not survive a prison sentence because of her addiction. Bessie testified that she had intended to retrieve ten dollars a local pimp had taken from her. She carried a gun only to scare him into returning her money. When Bessie knocked on his door, his companion, Big Eva, answered. In a fit of misplaced jealousy, Big Eva—more than twice Bessie's size—lunged at her. Bessie fired the gun, fearing for her life. Witnesses and the coroner's inquest corroborated Bessie's plea of self-defense, and her attorney anticipated acquittal. When Judge John B. McClernan read the guilty verdict,

Bessie moaned, screamed, threw herself on the floor, and lapsed into unconsciousness. Awaiting her sentence, which carried a possible ten years to life, Bessie was so hysterical and in such physical agony that doctors periodically gave her morphine to save her life. When Judge McClernan handed down a very harsh twenty-year sentence, it seemed to spectators that he might as well have sentenced her to death. Bessie entered Deer Lodge on June 20, 1901, and did not die in prison. She served half her sentence, much longer than she should have served with time for good behavior. She was finally paroled in 1911.

Edith Colby's Mistake

ASPIRING journalist Edith Colby came to Thompson Falls from Spokane in 1916 and took a job with the democratic *Independent-Enterprise*. Edith and others wrote some personal attacks on A. C. Thomas, chairman of the Republican County Central Committee, that were published in the paper. She and Thomas traded verbal insults, and Thomas accused Edith of loose morals. Enraged, Edith stole a loaded revolver that she showed to her boss, attorney A. S. Ainsworth, and her editor, John Manire. Manire showed her how to use the weapon and suggested that shooting Thomas would be good for the newspaper. The two men later testified that they had no idea Edith would actually pull the trigger. But she did. Edith met Thomas on the street and shot him three times. The coroner's inquest found that both Ainsworth and Manire shared the blame with Edith. All three were arrested. Burton K. Wheeler of Butte, later a well-known political figure, was the relentless special prosecutor. However, the court dropped all charges against Ainsworth, and the judge directed the jury to find Manire not guilty. Edith pled not guilty by reason of insanity, and her mother testified that mental illness ran in the family. Newspapers across the Northwest covered the spectacular murder trial. Edith's dramatic lapses into unconsciousness earned

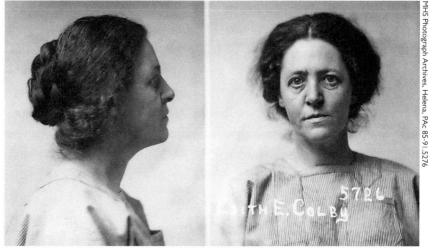

Edith Colby, mugshot, 1916

her no sympathy. Found guilty, she received ten to twelve years at Deer Lodge. Edith's attorneys appealed, claiming that Wheeler maligned Edith Colby's character during the trial and made public remarks that affected the verdict. The Supreme Court of Montana denied a new trial. Edith Colby served only two years at Deer Lodge, returned to newspaper work, and died in California in 1942.

Montana's Last Hanging

MONTANA has legally executed seventy-five individuals since Montana Territory carried out its first hanging in 1875. Montana's last hanging occurred in September 1943 when Philip J. Coleman Jr. was put to death in Missoula. At that time the law specified that executions be carried out in the county where the crime occurred. Coleman bludgeoned Carl Pearson to death and fatally stabbed his wife during an early-morning robbery at the couple's home in Lothrop at the western edge of Missoula County. Judge Albert Besancon sentenced Coleman to death for the first-degree murder of Mrs. Pearson, without a jury trial. His execution took place only forty-eight days after sentencing, the shortest amount of time between sentencing and hanging ever in Montana. While incarcerated and awaiting the execution, Coleman claimed to have killed twenty-three other persons in other states, beginning when he was fourteen. He named eight of his victims. The hanging took place inside the Missoula County jail. The trap-type gallows is today stored at the Fort Missoula Historical Museum. Remnants of Montana's violent past in the form of gallows lie scattered about the state on display in small museums. The most dramatic example sits in the Old Prison Museum at Deer Lodge in the burned-out W. A. Clark Theatre. The Ryegate gallows used in the 1938 hanging of W. Lee Simpson is on public display there. Its thirteen steps to the platform and the crossbeam with its dangling noose are chilling examples of western justice and a reminder of how it was done during much of Montana's judicial history.

Hurdy-Gurdy Houses

JOSEPHINE "CHICAGO JOE" AIREY opened Helena's first female-owned hurdy-gurdy house in 1867. Hurdy-gurdy houses, dating back to the California gold rush, were named for the hand organ—like an organ grinder used—that originally provided music in such places. For a dollar, a miner could buy a dance partner and afterward escort her to the bar for a free drink. By the time the hurdy-gurdies made their appearance in Montana, a piano or a three-piece orchestra had long replaced the hurdy-gurdy organ, but the name stuck. After fire destroyed Chicago Joe's first business, she opened Joe's Red Light Saloon in 1875 and imported ladies from Chicago to work for her. She had a reputation as a good businesswoman, but not everyone approved of her saloon. In fact, territorial legislation prohibited "hurdy gurdy houses and dancing saloons," but the law was usually ignored. Saloon proprietor Ulm Moller—a neighbor of Joe's—proved himself not guilty of running a hurdy-gurdy house in 1875 with the aid of Webster's dictionary. Moller's attorney proved that the saloon was not a hurdy-gurdy house because no such instrument had ever been seen there, nor was it a dancing saloon. After all, had anyone ever seen a saloon dance? A few years later, Republican district attorney William Hunt had Chicago Joe arrested and charged under this same law. It was impossible to find an objective jury in Helena, and so, with the aid of the dictionary, Joe was also acquitted. The next time elections came around, Hunt didn't run himself, but Joe campaigned door to door and successfully sabotaged his Republican protégé.

Sedition

MONTANA had one of the nation's harshest sedition laws, making it illegal to speak out against U.S. involvement in World War I. Among the dozens of people who went to prison for this crime, Janet Smith was the only woman who did time at Deer Lodge. She and her husband, William, ran the post office at Sayle south of Miles City and had a ranch in the Powder River country. Mrs. Smith was famous for her cooking and often fed dozens of cowboys at her table. She stood accused of bragging that if the people revolted, she would be the first one to shoulder a gun and get the president. She called the Red Cross a fake and said the disabled, insane, and convicts should be killed to save food instead of the government's restricting it from the rest of the population. The jury found her guilty. The judge gave her five to ten years, and she was taken from the courtroom sobbing. Her husband had also made seditious statements and was found guilty. Author Clemens P. Work in his book *Darkest Before Dawn* suggests that the isolation of ranchers like the Smiths made them particularly vulnerable, not realizing the implications of their casual talk. "In 1918," Work writes, "what was skeptical became unpatriotic, what was thrifty became miserly, and what was opinion became sedition." Janet Smith served twenty-six months before the Supreme Court reversed her conviction on the grounds that the language with which she was charged was not specific enough to convict her. William Smith was paroled at about the same time. What happened to the Smiths after their release has yet to be discovered.

Bootlegger Trail

No government policy failed so profoundly as did Prohibition, especially in Montana. First under state law in 1918 and then under the federal Volstad Act in 1919, Prohibition encouraged illegal activities and fostered the growth of organized crime. The term *bootlegger* comes from the moonshine peddler's practice of concealing illegal liquor in the top of his boot. Hoodwinking the revenue officer was often viewed as a game of cat and mouse, and tales of chases and near misses color local histories of the 1920s. Good whiskey came across the border from Canada, and the backroads route from Coutts (Coots), Alberta, to Great Falls became known as the Bootlegger Trail. But plenty of Montana moonshiners brewed whiskey, wine, and bath tub gin. There were tricks to rum running. Professional bootleggers—dangerous criminals who packed firearms and knew how to use them—drove Studebakers, Buick Roadmasters, and other touring cars. Local sheriffs drove what their counties could afford—the cheaper Model T's—which left county law enforcement eating dust. Bootleggers stayed on roads farthest from the county seats and close to neighboring county lines since one county had no jurisdiction over another. If a chase ensued across county lines, the law could not cross over. Federal agents, however, were a different story. Like professional criminals, they, too, drove big touring cars. They would lie in wait at bridges and strategic points. Ray Woods of Choteau County recalls many a time when a bootlegger's touring car got stuck fleeing from federal agents. His father would hitch up four horses to pull it out. Consequently, he always had a stash of whiskey, given as grateful payment.

Skunk Whiskey

MONTANA boasted many moonshiners during Prohibition, but one of them had a home brew with a very distinctive taste. Lyle Williams tells about this fellow who was a trapper by trade but made most of his living in the illegal whiskey trade. This old mountain man trapped mink, weasel, and skunk. The skunks were particularly prolific around his territory, and so he often had an abundance of skunk pelts. He would skin the animals and hang the pelts on the walls of his back porch to cure. Oftentimes he would have more than a hundred pelts hanging. This back porch had a trap door in the floor that led to the cellar. This was where the trapper kept his still and made his moonshine. One day he saw some strangers in his yard, and he feared the revenue officer was about to pay him a visit. He threw all the half-cured skunk pelts over the trap door. He let the men into his kitchen, and they asked if they could buy some moonshine. The trapper gave them the name of a prearranged go-between and knew that the agents would investigate further. But the revenue men had no idea that they were standing not four feet over the basement still. The men looked all around, but stayed away from the smelly skunk pelts. They finally went on their way, much to the trapper's relief. Later on, one of the trapper's customers noted that he could always tell the moonshine that came from the trapper's still. It tasted faintly of skunk.

Legal Beer

EIGHT months before the official end of Prohibition, patrons at Walkers Bar in Butte raised glasses of beer in celebration.

For years a sign in the bar (which is still in business adjacent the Metals Bank Building) read, "The only place in the United States that served Draught Beer over the bar April 8, 1933." President Franklin Roosevelt gave the repeal of Prohibition top priority because traffic in illegal liquor fostered so much criminal activity. Roosevelt knew its repeal would take time. So when he took office in 1933, he signed the Cullen-Harrison Act legalizing beverages with an alcohol content of 3.2 percent. Twenty states, including Montana, legalized 3.2 beer. The law took effect on April 7, and within twenty-four hours, the nation consumed 1.5 million barrels of beer. Montana enjoyed its 3.2 beer until the Twenty-first Amendment repealing Prohibition took effect eight months later on December 5. Although Montana was one of twenty states legalizing 3.2 beer, except for Walkers in Butte, beer didn't magically appear in local Montana bars. While state beer licenses brought in seventy-three thousand dollars in the first two days, legal beer only trickled into the state. The first shipment of 3.2 Pabst left Milwaukee on April 7, the very same day it became legal. A new refrigerated warehouse at the Northern Pacific Railway yards in Helena waited to store it for distribution. But it was five days before Helena got its first taste of legal beer. With 1.5 million barrels of beer consumed nationwide in the first twenty-four hours after the signing of the Cullen-Harrison Act, Walkers could not have been the country's only outlet. The question is: how did Walkers get its first legal 3.2 beer at a moment's notice?

Birdie (Bertie) Brown

THE rutted road was a familiar one to Fergus County locals during the days of Prohibition. You had to be careful—bad hooch could cause blindness and even death. Those looking for a place to party knew to point their cars toward Black Butte and Birdie Brown's place. She was as nice a woman as they come, and her still—according to locals—produced some of the best moonshine in the country. Birdie was among a very small number of young African American women who homesteaded alone in Montana. She was in her twenties when she settled in the Lewistown area in 1898. She later homesteaded along Brickyard Creek in 1913. During Prohibition in the 1920s, Birdie carved a niche for herself. Her neat homestead where she lived with her cat was a place of warm hospitality. Birdie's parlor was legendary. In May 1933, just months before the end of Prohibition and Birdie's livelihood, the revenue officer came around and warned her to stop her brewing. But as Birdie multitasked, dry cleaning some garments with gasoline and tending what would be her last batch of hooch, the gasoline exploded in her face. She lived a few hours, long enough to request that someone take care of her beloved pet. But the cat that followed her everywhere was never found. Birdie's once orderly homestead now lies in a state of collapse, tragically transformed into a ghost of its former self. Roundup artist Jane Stanfel, who has painted Birdie's homestead, makes a strange observation. Although it's been nearly eighty years since Birdie's passing, every so often someone catches a glimpse of a black cat perched in her parlor window.

Homesteading Tales

Homestead Act

THE Enlarged Homestead Act of 1909 doubled free land from 160 acres to 320. Homesteaders came by the thousands, and by 1910, agriculture in Montana surpassed mining in both numbers of people working farms and in the revenue it generated. Unusual amounts of rainfall produced abundant harvests, and this trick of Mother Nature fooled farmers into believing that Montana was truly a paradise. In 1909, total wheat production reached almost eleven million bushels, but in the "miracle year" of 1915, Montana farms produced more than forty-two million bushels. The unusual bounty ended after 1918 when drought destroyed crops and wind turned over-plowed topsoil into dust storms. Homesteaders who took up claims in central and eastern Montana found timber and water scarce. Some traveled twenty-five miles to cut fence posts and firewood. Some dug their own coal to keep warm in brutal winter cold. Between 1921 and 1925, half the farmers in Montana lost their farms. Of the eighty-two thousand immigrants who came to Montana to homestead, seventy thousand left before 1925. Between 1919 and 1925, farming ceased on some two million acres, and homesteaders abandoned eleven thousand farms—about 20 percent of the state's total. Half of Montana's farmers lost their land.

Even so, agriculture remains Montana's backbone and its largest essential industry. Today, farms and ranches make up 66 percent of the state's ninety-three million acres. Statistics show, however, that the number of farms and ranches has dropped by almost 50 percent since 1920, when there were 57,700 farms in Montana. As of 2008, there were only 29,500, roughly half as many. But it is true that, according to the U.S. Department of Agriculture, there are still three head of cattle for every person in Montana.

Jonathan and Almira Manlove

THE tiny homestead cabin that sits across the railroad tracks at the southeast corner of East Helena originally sat in the middle of town at Kennedy Park. The East Helena Kiwanis Club disassembled the cabin and moved it with care in 1981. The 1864 cabin was the first home of Jonathan and Almira Manlove, who were making their way with a wagon train en route to Oregon. The emigrants stopped to rest under a stand of cottonwood trees and repair their wagons. Almira was pregnant and did not feel up to traveling farther, so they stayed in the Prickly Pear Valley. They built their cabin, planted potatoes, and hauled wagonloads of produce to the early mining camps. The cottonwood trees are still known as Manlove Grove, and part of the townsite of East Helena was once the Manloves' potato field. Jonathon had been a schoolteacher, miner, freighter, and trader and always did a lot of traveling. Almira Manlove raised nine children, who helped her run the farm. She pursued her own interests in photography and taxidermy. An accomplished taxidermist, Almira displayed her bird and animal subjects in a handsome, specially made cabinet in the lobby of Samuel Hauser's First National Bank in Helena. Historic photographs also show her work displayed with the first exhibits of the Montana Historical Society in the basement of the new State Capitol in the early twentieth century. The Manloves were among the first settlers in

Lewis and Clark County to put down roots. Their cabin recalls the perseverance and varied talents of Montana's first pioneers.

Laura Etta Smalley

AMONG the thousands who came to Montana to take advantage of the Enlarged Homestead Act were courageous and independent single women. One was Laura Etta Smalley, a woman determined to carve out a place of her own. Single women could not claim homesteads in Canada, and so Laura Etta, an Edmonton teacher, did her homework. Over the Easter break in 1910, she took the train to Inverness, Montana. Arriving in the middle of the night, she found a room in the unfinished hotel, and early the next morning she drove out with the land locator and chose her homestead. Then she took the night train to Havre, was first in line to register her claim, and returned to Canada before Easter break was over. She

Grace Binks (left) and Margaret Majors pose with a homestead shack near Sumatra, eighty miles northeast of Billings as the crow flies.

finished out the school year and then returned to Montana, bought and furnished a tiny, ready-made house, and had it moved on two wagons the twenty-six miles to her homestead. She planted her acreage and returned to Canada to teach in the fall. Soon she got a job teaching in Inverness, and a few years later married William Bangs. They moved to his homestead. When drought, grasshoppers, and bankruptcy forced hundreds to leave Montana, Laura and her family persevered. But then the bank foreclosed and William lost his homestead. The family of six moved to Laura's abandoned claim. They squeezed into the old fourteen-by-twenty-foot claim shack. Through the 1930s, the family weathered the Great Depression. After Laura died in 1973, her grandson took over her original claim. The homestead, still in the family, has been recognized as one of Montana's Centennial Farms and Ranches.

Annie Morgan

LEGEND has it that African American Annie Morgan was a cook for General George Armstrong Custer. After the Battle of the Little Bighorn, she eventually made her way to Philipsburg in Granite County. This part of the story has been disputed, and Annie's past is uncertain. However, it is a fact that Granite County attorney David Durfee hired her to take his uncle—who had a severe drinking problem—to an abandoned fox farm on Upper Rock Creek to dry out. Annie cared for the uncle, and when he eventually went his own way, she stayed on, filing on a homestead. One day in 1894, Annie happened upon a local character named Joseph Case lying on the banks of Rock Creek gravely ill with typhoid. Case was a Civil War veteran from New Jersey who made a living catching fish to sell in Philipsburg, where he was known as "Fisher Jack." Annie nursed Jack through the illness, and to repay her, Jack stayed on to fence Annie's homestead. The pair developed a mutual affection, and when the fence was done, Jack stayed on. Annie died in

1914, and both she and Jack are buried in the Philipsburg cemetery. The Forest Service has beautifully restored Annie's cabin. In the process, workers discovered a curious bundle hidden in the upper door frame. Bits of red string, a soap wrapper, and other items consistent with the bundles carried by African root doctors suggest that perhaps Annie carried these traditions to the Montana frontier. She certainly proved her skills at doctoring. The Morgan-Case Homestead* is available for short-term rental by lottery through the Missoula Ranger District.

Those Old-time Dances

AMONG homesteading settlements and mining camps, dances were a favorite pastime. They might be held in a community hall, a school, or a barn. If the facility had no piano, one would be brought in from someone's home or a church. A common pre-dance activity was preparing the dance floor. Adults would spread cornmeal on the floor boards and all the children would spend the afternoon skating around to polish the wood. People sometimes came on horseback or brought their families by wagon from as far as forty miles away. Guests brought their own liquor to be dispensed at the host's discretion. A two-gallon dance was a small gathering, while a twenty-five-gallon dance was an occasion to remember. The hostess served three meals: supper, midnight supper, and breakfast. The fiddler's tuning up signaled the beginning of the dance. The grand march always came first. The march involved winding in single or double file, and four abreast, then under an arch with women to the right and men to the left at the direction of the caller. A quadrille usually followed the grand march. This was a square dance of sorts. There was much foot-stamping and floors needed to be very sturdy. Dancers whirled and twirled their partners to the waltz and the polka. The midnight meal was served during a lull so that dancers, callers, and musicians could catch their breath.

Soon the fiddler would again tune up and the dance would start anew. Breakfast, served in the wee hours of the morning, signaled the dance had come to an end.

Evelyn Cameron Scandalizes Miles City

PHOTOGRAPHER Evelyn Cameron is a recent inductee into the Gallery of Outstanding Montanans in the State Capitol. Evelyn was born in England and raised to be a proper English lady. But once she created a real scandal. Evelyn's husband was a noted ornithologist and naturalist, but he didn't care much for their ranch. That was all right with Evelyn, who enjoyed the physical work. Chores and most everything from making bread to milking cows and working the horses fell to her. She took to wearing a divided riding skirt that allowed her to ride astride rather than sidesaddle. The long skirt was much like modern culottes. Victorian women, however, did not wear pants. And when Evelyn first rode into Miles City in the dark blue divided skirt she had ordered from California,

One of the Buckley sisters of eastern Montana dismounting, wearing an Evelyn Cameron—introduced divided skirt, 1914

oh, the scandal it caused. Although the skirt was so full it looked like an ordinary dress when she was on foot, on horseback the division was obvious. Law enforcement warned her not to ride on the streets in town or she might be arrested. But town was forty-eight miles from her ranch, and riding sidesaddle could only be done on a very slow and gentle horse. Evelyn would not ride what she called old "dead heads." She became convinced that riding in a man's saddle stride-legged was the only safe way for a woman to ride. Before long, other women took to the divided skirt and it became an accepted way of dressing for women not only on the streets of Miles City but also on homesteads, farms, and ranches across Montana.

The Ellis Family's Wagon

HOMESTEAD boosters in the 1890s enticed the Herbert Ellis family to leave their Iowa farm and settle in North Dakota. Several years later, in 1901, their cattle died and they decided to move on to Washington. Herbert built a tiny wooden house he set on wheels and hitched to four horses. Herbert and Rose Mary Ellis, their five children, and Herbert's brother Robert traveled in the wagon house and camped along the way. Daughter Goldie, thirteen years old at the time, left a written account of the family's adventures. When they reached Livingston, Montana, two of their horses died, and they could go no farther. They stayed, living for a time in the wagon house. Herbert got a job at Yellowstone National Park, and in 1902, the family bought a small two-room house on South Eighth Street. Herbert took the wagon off its wheels and attached it to the house. Gradually, the house grew around the wagon, until the wagon disappeared under the roof and among the walls. A century later, in 2002, a family newly arrived in Livingston bought the property. A portion of the house was in bad shape, so the new owners began to remove the old walls and roof. And there they discovered the one-hundred-year-old wagon with its green-painted wooden walls, black-trimmed roof, and hitching rings exactly as it was when Herbert Ellis placed it there. Great-grandchildren of the Ellises still residing in Livingston had heard the story of the wagon and always wondered if it was fact or myth. Not only did its discovery solve the mystery, but family items were also found, including a tiny pair of children's shoes and a portrait of the Ellis children that was returned to family members.

Homestead Horror!

A PLENTYWOOD rancher once told of a childhood experience that made a lasting impression. Before the Rural Electrification Administration brought electricity to many ranches in the late 1930s, the New Deal's Agricultural Adjustment Administration helped Montana farmers by channeling some ten million dollars' worth of contract money into the desperate economy. Some families who benefited from this new money splurged on automobiles. This particular family was proud of their new car, and in the evenings they would go visiting. One warm spring evening as the family returned home after such a visit, they drove into the driveway. As they approached the dark house, the headlights flashed upon the attic window, and they saw a white figure moving back and forth in the light. As was the family custom, the children drew straws to see who had to go into the dark house first to light the kerosene lamp. The short straw fell to this youngster. He was terrified, but his father told him to get to it, and so he approached the house with weak knees. Instructed to discover what was in the window, the youngster slowly made his way up the stairs, taking the treads one by one. He thought he would faint he was so scared. Finally he got to the top stair, took a deep breath, and flung the door open. Relief flooded through him. During the cold winter months, his mother used the attic to hang the laundry, and hanging in the window was a forgotten pair of long johns swaying in the breeze.

Missoula's Garden Roots

CLARENCE PRESCOTT came to Montana in 1878 to work for his prominent uncle, C. P. Higgins. Prescott became a state legislator, county commissioner, sheriff, and chief of police. He took up a homestead at the base of Mount Sentinel in 1891 and planted a vast orchard of plum, cherry, pear, and apple trees. He proved up, gained title to the land in 1896, and in 1898 moved with his wife, Julia, and their children to the rural homestead. Prescott built an eleven-room, Queen Anne–style residence modeled after Julia's childhood home in Pennsylvania. As the Prescotts raised their four children, they witnessed encroaching progress. Their homestead was adjacent to the new state college. They could barely see the clock tower on Main Hall, the first campus building, for all the trees in their orchard. But into the 1900s, the campus grew up around them. The Prescotts' orchard became a little island of green, bolstering Missoula's claim as the Garden City. Clarence Jr., the couple's oldest child and only son, moved back to the family farm when his father died in 1939. An auto mechanic by trade, he never married and lived a long life on the property. In 1945, Clarence leased forty acres to the university. The School of Forestry used the land as a tree nursery and pharmaceutical gardens. In 1955, the University of Montana purchased the land but gave Clarence life tenancy of the house and the right to harvest the fruit of the adjacent trees. Clarence died in 1993 at age one hundred. Prescott House*, beautifully restored, now hosts prestigious university events and receptions. It is a rare link to Missoula's early agricultural roots.

Bless the Beasts

Wild Horse Island

WILD HORSE ISLAND in Flathead Lake preserves an endangered prairie environment and encompasses some 2,100 acres. Over the decades, horses, mule deer, Virginia turkeys, bighorn sheep, and a few human residents have been imported there. Its unusual history goes back to local tribes who used the island as a natural corral to keep their horses safe from other tribes. The first written record dates to 1854 when a herd of about seventy horses was reported there. The island opened to homesteaders in 1910. Its pine forests and prairie grassland lured settlers who planted fruit trees and tried to farm. But extreme isolation soon led to abandonment. Ownership passed to wealthy easterners. Colonel Almond White planned a boys' school and resort on the island. He later tried to market his villa sites as homes but died penniless in 1923. In 1931, Reverend Robert Edgington built a dude ranch on the island, but his tragic drowning ended this venture. The stone chimney of his Hiawatha Lodge is the only reminder. In 1943, the island's new owner rounded up eight wild horses to sell. Wranglers loaded them onto a small barge and tied them to a central ring. A wave flooded one side and the horses crowded together on the opposite side, causing the barge to flip. One man dove underwater and cut all eight horses free. The horses swam back to the island and disappeared. Severe winter in 1955 reduced the herd of one hundred to only a few. Montana Fish, Wildlife, and Parks imports and maintains the half dozen wild mustangs that now run free on the island, which became a state park in 1978.

Cats Earned Their Keep

WHEN did the first cats come to Montana? Rats came to the trading posts and camps very early, hitching rides in the staples and goods brought for consumption and for trade. Protection of precious supplies from invading pests was critical. Jesuit priests made the same discovery. Father Nicholas Pointe, one of the founders of St. Mary's Mission* in the Bitterroot Valley in 1841, drew a sketch of the Jesuits in a primitive grass shelter. The lively scene shows six priests and lay brothers surrounded by their boxes of goods. A dog and two black cats frolic among the men. This early scene suggests that the Jesuits brought the first cats to Montana when they established St. Mary's, the first Catholic mission in the entire Northwest. In 1850, the Jesuits closed the original mission but returned to rebuild it in 1866. Father Anthony Ravalli had been with the founding Jesuits in the 1840s. He also returned to the Bitterroot to design a new church. Ravalli was a physician, pharmacist, talented architect, and artist. He also had a great fondness for cats. As he worked on the interior furnishings of St. Mary's Mission Church—the one that still stands at Stevensville today—he often improvised materials. From his writing we know that Father Ravalli made the brushes for his paintings in the church from the tail hair of Tomaso, his favorite cat. These were not Montana's only feline residents. Pierre Choteau's inventory of possessions and supplies at Fort Benton* in 1851 lists horses, mules, bulls, oxen, and pigs. Last on the list is one cat, valued at $5. Translate that into modern currency, and the cat was worth $129.

Dynamite

HE just showed up one day on a street corner in Butte. No one knew where he came from; he was just there, a big yellow and white collie dog with some shepherd thrown in. He adopted this particular corner, and it was his home for a number of years. The traffic cop named him Dynamite. He had fondness for men in uniform, children, and T-bone steaks served at the back doors of Butte's restaurants. In the winter, passersby could see Dynamite curled up at the feet of the traffic cop on duty, who directed traffic standing upon a steam-heated grill. Dynamite loved fires. At the first alarm, Dynamite would rush to the scene with an uncanny sense of exactly where the fire was, often beating the firemen there. He barked and wagged his tail until the blaze was out. Then the hook and ladder took him back to his street corner. Dynamite always knew when there was a baseball game south of town at Clark Park and jumped aboard the southbound streetcar. Arriving at the gate, he would stride through and trot onto the field like one of the players, to a rousing cheer. Dynamite rode the streetcar to Columbia Gardens with the children of Butte on weekly Children's Day. No other dog was allowed to ride public transportation. But the years crept by, and Dynamite felt the winter cold. In 1927, as passengers celebrated their departure on the annual midwinter Union Pacific special to Los Angeles, Dynamite hopped the streetcar to the depot, boarded the train for sunny California, and never returned to Butte.

The Ghost Horse Named Paint

ONCE there was a bay pinto born on the prairie to an old mare who had given many foals to her Crow owner. The horse's name was Paint. In the five years he lived with the Crow, he learned the feel of a man on his back and the ways of the buffalo hunt. One night as his people camped along Painted Robe Creek in today's

Montana's "favorite" artist, Charlie Russell, on Monte, early 1880s

Golden Valley County, Blackfeet crept into the sleeping camp to steal the horses. Paint felt a man on his back and began to run. Gunfire shattered the night. Paint felt the man go slack, and then Paint ran alone. When the horses stopped running, the Blackfeet saw that one man was missing. Their leader, Bad Wound, looked over the captive horses and noted Paint was good and strong. But then he saw the dried blood on his back. He drew his Henry rifle and fired at Paint. The horse fell to his knees and rolled on his side. Bad Wound wanted to send the dead warrior a good horse to take him on his last journey. But later Bad Wound saw Paint among the herd, dried blood on his head and neck, but otherwise sound. The bullet had gone completely through his neck, and Paint lived. But he was the steed of a dead man, and no one would ride a ghost horse. The following spring, some whites came to the Blackfeet to buy horses. Bad Wound sold Paint to a young boy named Charlie Russell. Paint, whom Russell renamed Monte, was his favorite horse, and the two were inseparable until the horse died of extreme old age twenty-five years later.

Expensive Cats

 HARRIET SANDERS tells a wonderful tale in her reminiscence *Biscuits and Badmen*. When she and her husband moved to Virginia City in the earliest days of the mining camp, commodities of all kinds were at a premium, delivered by ox team or mule train from great distances and at great expense. One day a merchant arrived with a peculiar cargo: a whole wagonload of cats! The cats had traveled five hundred miles in boxes. This living merchandise was important because Virginia City had a serious problem with mice. Mice had arrived with freight from the East, and the mining camp was overrun with them. Food items were so precious that this infestation was very serious. There were no cats in the region, and these, the merchant knew, would bring premium prices. So he boxed them up and brought them from Salt Lake City. The first cat brought five dollars. But when the merchant saw that the cats were in such great demand, he sold the next for ten and then twenty dollars, each cat fetching a bigger price than the one before. And when he came to the very last mewing cats, no one wanted to buy them because they were the last choice. "Ah," said the merchant, "but these cats are the most special, and I have saved them for last. These are the best mousers of them all!" With that, the merchant fetched a price of forty dollars for the last ones. Soon Virginia City was rid of its problem. Descendants of those first cats are without a doubt still catching mice in Alder Gulch.

Shep

FORT BENTON'S River and Plains Society tells how in the summer of 1936, a sheepherder became ill and was brought to the hospital in Fort Benton. A dog followed his flock of sheep into town and hung around the hospital, where a kindly nun fed him. The herder died, and his relatives asked that his body be sent back East. The undertaker put the casket on the train, and the engine pulled away. The dog followed along the tracks until the train sped away, beginning a five-and-a-half year vigil. Day after day, the dog—named Shep by locals—met every passenger train, eying each person who got off. Neither heat nor rain nor snow prevented Shep from meeting those trains. Irene Schanche Bowker recalls that her father, depot agent Tony Schanche, coaxed the dog into the depot from the cold station platform. After gaining his trust, Schanche taught him tricks. Shep's fame spread, and people came to photograph him, try to make friends, and possibly adopt him. But Shep was a one-man dog. The bond he had formed with the herder was simply the most important thing to him. Although railroad employees gave Shep food and shelter, that was all he wanted, except his master's return. Time took its toll. On January 12, 1942, stiff-legged and deaf, Shep failed to hear the whistle as the 10:17 approached the depot that cold winter morning. Witnesses said he turned to look when the engine was almost upon him, moved to get out of the way, and slipped on the icy rails. His long vigil ended. Two days later, Shep had a grand funeral. Boy Scouts played taps, and a local minister read a moving eulogy on man's best friend. Loving citizens laid Shep to rest on the bluff overlooking the station where his long wait had come to a sad end.

Custer's Dogs

GENERAL GEORGE CUSTER had his faults, but one characteristic makes him more likable. Custer loved dogs. He owned as many as forty and took them with him everywhere. Historian Brian Dippie wrote that Custer's dogs "accompanied him on hunts and campaigns; they arranged themselves at his feet, rested their heads on his lap, shared his bed and his food, got under foot, made nuisances of themselves, but never lost their special place in his affection. They were like people to him." His dogs adored him, too. When Maida, one of his favorites, was killed during a buffalo hunt, Custer wrote a rather bad, but very heartfelt, poem to her. During the Black Hills expedition in 1874, Custer wrote to his wife that his dogs surrounded him and that his favorite, Tuck, a tall, light-colored deerhound, slept at the head of his bed. On June 12, 1876, two weeks before the Little Bighorn battle, Custer again wrote: "Tuck regularly comes when I am writing, and lays her head on the desk, rooting up my hand with her long nose until I consent to stop and notice her." Several dogs including Custer's beloved Tuck broke away from the pack train and followed their master into the famous battle. Indian witnesses claimed that Custer was easy to spot among the fray because of the tall, light-colored dog that stayed at his side until the last moments. The Cheyenne warrior Wooden Leg recalled a dog on Custer Hill, and soldiers saw a dog on a distant rise, but none was seen again. Tuck was not listed among the casualties. We will never know for sure what became of her or her renegade companions.

A Cowboy and His Horse

THE *Great Falls Tribune* of August 30, 1951, related a heart-warming true tale of a cowboy and his horse. Henry Haughian and Buck were rounding up cattle in the rugged outback country of the Sheep Mountains north of Miles City in Dawson County. Buck, usually a surefooted horse, probably got to daydreaming and stumbled on the steep hillside. Henry had no time to jump off. He was caught beneath the horse as Buck rolled down the hill. The fall frightened Buck, who got up, shook himself, shied away, and took off down the hill as fast as he could go. But when Buck got over his fright, he realized that his master was missing. He climbed back up the rocky hillside, searching for him. He found Henry lying unconscious on the slope. Buck then climbed to the top of the hill and stood sentinel there. No one knows how long he must have waited, motionless on that hilltop. Finally, sometime later, two sheepherders happened along and saw the horse silhouetted against the Montana sky. They noticed the empty saddle right away and made their way to the riderless horse. Once the men reached the top of the hill, Buck led them down the steep incline to the spot where Henry lay, still unconscious. The men carried Henry to their truck and took him to the hospital. Henry suffered three broken bones and extensive bruises but recovered from his ordeal. The story proves that humans and their animal companions have special bonds. Or maybe it proves that horses know where their next meal comes from. Whatever the explanation, Henry never forgot Buck because Buck did not forget him.

And the Children

Homer Thomas

HOMER THOMAS was eight years old when he came with his family to Montana Territory from Illinois. It was almost Christmas when Homer wrote a letter to his grandmother. "I am glad you didn't come with us," he wrote, "you could not have stood it; [the trip] was mighty hard." Homer described Virginia City as a poor place where the miners dressed in old, dirty, and ragged clothes. He wished especially for apples and cider, something not found in Montana. Homer's longing for Illinois comes through in his words, "I expect this will be a great country someday, but I don't care for that, just as soon as I can get enough gold, I bet you I am coming back." But Homer did not return to Illinois. A few years later, the family suffered tragedy when Indians scalped Homer's uncle William Thomas and ten-year-old cousin Charley at Sawyer's Cutoff near present-day Greycliff while they were en route to join the family. (One of Charley's small, worn boots survives in the Montana Historical Society's museum collection.) Homer eventually followed his father in the milling and feed business and later helped found the mining camp of Monarch. But that 1864 Christmas letter to his grandma, preserved in the Montana Historical Society archives, has a nostalgia unusual for an eight-year-old. "Well, Grandmother," he wrote toward the end of his letter, "it is pretty near Christmas time and I do not expect to get many things this year, for it is not like home, because old Santa Claus does not come out here to give children things, because he thinks all the children too smart to come to this old place. Well I can do without any nice toys this year, but I want you to save me some nice things so I can have them when I come back home." But the years passed and Homer Thomas stayed in Montana. Illinois faded to become a childhood memory.

Children in the Mining Camps

CHILDREN who spent time in the mining camps of Montana faced numerous dangers. Typhoid and cholera plagued mining camps because miners quickly polluted the water source. But measles, whooping cough, and diphtheria also invaded the communities. In 1889, diphtheria in the great silver camp of Elkhorn, for example, claimed almost all the children. During that same year, Harry Walton, nine, and Albin Nelson, ten, somehow escaped diphtheria, but they found a quicksilver container full of black powder. Adults filled these containers to detonate for community celebrations like the Fourth of July, and someone had overlooked this one. The boys managed to explode it and blew themselves to bits. They share a grave in the small, quaint cemetery up the mountainside. In all mining camps, mining-related accidents, mine shafts, and explosives posed real dangers. But of all the mining camps, the metropolitan industrial giant of Butte was probably the most dangerous place for youngsters. Growing up in Butte made children tough and unusually daring. They seemed to thrive in the polluted air and unsanitary conditions frequently noted in reports to the Board of Health. One Butte native who grew up there in the 1930s and 1940s recalled that mine officials came around to his elementary school and showed the kids what a blasting cap was, warned them not to pick one up, and showed them the explosive inside. After the lecture, every boy went out in search of caps. They learned to pour the powder into a bottle with a wick, put it on the train tracks, preferably on a trestle, and hope it would explode as a train passed by. Children lost limbs to this form of play, but danger made the game that much more fun.

Arline Allen's Embarrassing Innuendo

THE Allen family long operated one of Helena's most popular livery stables, the Allen Livery* at Ewing and Breckenridge. The former stable has a long and colorful history and is Helena's best-preserved reminder of this vital business. Its many "ghost signs" are also remarkably preserved. By 1867, William H. Allen established the business on his rich mining claim, where he picked gold nuggets out of the dirt. Allen's nephew, Joseph Allen, soon arrived to help out and eventually took over the business. Joseph built the current stone and brick stable around 1885. Contrary to popular belief, the upstairs never in its long history housed prostitution. Rather, lodging rooms accommodated the livery's hostlers and stablemen. Joseph Allen and his wife, Lurlie, had a daughter, Arline, who grew up around her father's horses. She and her friends never learned to ride sidesaddle but rode astride and wore divided riding skirts like other Montana women. Arline and her friends followed the trails all over the hills and had many adventures. But in 1912, when Arline was sixteen, both her mother and father died. Arline went to live with her grandmother in Virginia. She had a hard time because girls there never rode astride but only sidesaddle. She found horseback riding and ice skating in long full skirts terribly confining and longed to put on her Montana divided riding skirt. Shocked, her grandmother would not allow it. On her first ice skating date in Virginia, Arline said to the young man, "If I could just take this skirt off, I could really show you something!" Arline spent the rest of her life trying to live that one down.

Gold Fever

CHILDREN, like their parents, caught the gold fever. Traveling west with other families, they heard the tall tales of gold so plentiful you could shake it out of the sagebrush. But once arrived, they realized Montana's primitive camps were not as they had imagined. Five-year-old James Sanders, son of Wilbur and Harriet Sanders, crossed the plains with the Henry Edgerton family from Ohio to Montana. James heard the excited talk about the great gold camp at Bannack and Montana's golden gulches. After weeks of travel, the family at last arrived at the far-famed camp of Bannack. As the wagons entered the mining camp, James looked around at the ugly settlement. Everywhere he looked he saw the dirt churned up and piled high. There was not a single proper building, but poorly built cabins and tents straggled haphazardly along Grasshopper Creek. James well expressed what the adults were thinking but did not dare say. James observed with disappointment, "I fink Bangup is a humbug." Ten-year-old Mary "Mollie" Sheehan saw it a bit differently. She and her family arrived at Bannack as the first rumors of a new strike at Alder Gulch began to circulate. Her father, James, freighted the first load of goods to Virginia City and returned to take his family there. The Sheehans followed the trampled ground in the wake of stampeding miners. As the mule team panted up the last hill, the Sheehans stopped to let them rest. Mollie hopped down from the wagon, grabbed a stick, and wrote her name in the dirt, declaring to her father's amusement, "I stake my claim."

Montana's Second Book

MONTANA'S first published book was Thomas Dimsdale's *Vigilantes of Montana*. Do you know what Montana's second published book was? There are only three known copies of a little volume entitled *A Trip to the States in 1865*. Its author was sixteen-year-old

J. Allen Hosmer, the son of district court and supreme court judge Hezekiah Hosmer. Young Hosmer recorded the trip in his diary. We learn that it took a week to reach the head of navigation on the Yellowstone and forty-four days' river travel to get from Montana Territory to Iowa, the closest state. Printed on common newsprint, the book had butcher paper over its cardboard cover. Hand whip-stitching bound the ninety-four pages, printed one page at a time on a hand press. Young Hosmer was the author, editor, printer, and binder of the little book. No wonder there are only a few copies. The price of the book was a dollar in gold dust. J. Allen Hosmer came west with his family in 1864 and made the trip described in his book the following year. He returned to Virginia City and became clerk of the court and studied law under his father. The family moved to California in 1872, and Allen later served as prosecuting attorney in San Francisco and San Joaquin County. He died in 1907, just months after his appointment to the Supreme Court of California. Thus he followed closely in his father's footsteps. The record of the family's journey is not so remarkable in itself, but its preservation as the second book written and published in Montana makes it very special.

Smoking Cure

MANY Montanans have fond, and not so fond, childhood memories of Virginia City. Eileen Yeager, who grew up there in the 1890s, tells a story in the Madison County history *Trails and Trials* about games she and her sister Mary made up to amuse themselves. One was called "Bob and Bill." This game involved gathering old chewed cigar butts from behind a certain barn. Each girl had a cigar box that she filled with the old stogies. They had made a sidewalk of scrap wood in the backyard, and beginning at opposite ends, they sauntered toward each other, dressed in their dad's old hats. They met in the middle and took turns. Eileen would say, "Hello Bill." Mary answered, "Hello, Bob." They had a set dialogue, and after a bit, Eileen would say, "Would you like a cigar?" and open her cigar box. Each would take a stogie, light up, and saunter down the sidewalk, puffing away. Then they would switch roles and do it again. One day, Mary must have forgotten and inhaled. She keeled right over, and Eileen ran into the house announcing dramatically, "Mama, Mary is dead!" Their mother rushed out to find Mary violently ill. She called the doctor, who immediately asked Eileen, "What have you been smoking?" Eileen showed him the box of damp, chewed cigar butts. This time her mother keeled over. Eileen didn't understand why her mother fainted, but the spanking made a lasting impression. Thus Eileen quit smoking at the age of six, and neither she nor Mary ever took it up again.

Begging Children

On December 31, 1864, the *Montana Post*—Montana's first newspaper published in Virginia City—noted what it termed "a flagrant and wanton instance of unnatural conduct of parents toward their children." While most children had parents who watched over them and gave them rules to follow, some unfortunate youngsters in the mining camps were in desperate need of nonexistent social services. On this occasion, three little sisters begged at the door of James Fergus in Virginia City. The *Montana Post* reported that two of the girls were ages ten and twelve, and the third, in the arms of the oldest girl, was an infant. The children wore little more than calico slips and shivered in the December cold. They gave their last name as Canary. Authorities quickly learned that the girls' father was a gambler in nearby Nevada City and their mother had not been seen for several days. Mrs. Fergus and other women in Virginia City gave the children food and clothing before reluctantly returning them to their gambler father in Nevada City. There was no other alternative. The *Montana Post* could only publicly chastise the parents, noting that the laws of man that they so audaciously violated should be applied and stern justice meted out to them. The paper also suggested that an income tax be enacted so that prisoners and the destitute—like these three children—could receive some relief. Historical evidence suggests that the identity of the twelve-year-old was Martha Canary, who grew up to become one of Montana's most infamous characters: Calamity Jane.

Bad Boys

FRANK DAVEY had the patent on the Garnet claim, and so he owned most of the land upon which the town of Garnet* was built. He operated Garnet's general store and ran the post office. Mr. Davey had an icehouse with secret compartments built into the back wall. There the gold would be stored before the stage could take it down to Bearmouth. Mr. Davey's store held all kinds of merchandise, such as shoes, hardware, canned goods, and meat. He had a stockpile of flour and sugar that he would sell only in emergencies. This policy angered residents, and Mr. Davey, in his stodgy three-piece suit, was not well liked. His store, however, was a main attraction, and the children of Garnet, especially the older boys, liked to hang out there. The boys played mean tricks on Frank Davey. It was no wonder he kept a watchful eye on his merchandise. He displayed the penny candy behind a glass case, away from little fingers. The boys would place their order, and Mr. Davey would fill the sack. When he plunked it down on the counter, the boys would snatch it, put down rocks instead of money, and run away. Mr. Davey threatened to tell their parents, but he never did. He secretly thought it was amusing. Once, the boys found a three-piece suit like Mr. Davey always wore, stuffed it with straw, and hung the effigy on the hotel's flagpole. The ultimate insult was that Mr. Davey also owned the hotel and the flagpole. Mr. Davey was the last living resident in Garnet when he died in 1947, but some believe he never left. One recent summer day in Garnet, several children and their mother reported a suspicious man around the icehouse, scaring the children. Staff went to investigate, but the man was nowhere to be seen. The visitors' description fit Mr. Davey perfectly, right down to his three-piece suit.

Summers in Garnet

In the 1920s, Elizabeth Farmer Smith spent three summers at the mining camp of Garnet, where her father was an engineer. Elizabeth's recollections—stored at the Montana Historical Society's Research Center—tell us much about children in Montana's mining camps. Elizabeth writes about the fun she and the other children had sliding down the mine dumps on pieces of tin, riding in the empty ore cars as the miners pushed them back into the mine to reload, and watching her father scrape the mercury tables at the end of the day. The balls of mercury would catch the gold. When enough had accumulated, the blacksmith would melt the tiny pieces in a vat, leaving a blob of shiny gold at the bottom. The children found a swimming hole deep in the woods, and they

Montana Historical Society Photograph Archives, Helena, PAc 79-60.6

Almeda Farmer and her daughters Elizabeth (standing) and Winnifred at Bearmouth, near Garnet, in 1923, posing with their 1922 Buick

could always recognize it by the luscious carpet of watercress covering the surface. On the Fourth of July, all of Garnet turned out for the community dance. Elizabeth's family had a 1922 Buick that her mother learned to drive. Few women at that time learned to drive, and it was an unusual feat of which the family was very proud. But the horse-drawn stage to Bearmouth still operated, and three times a week it would bring the Farmer family a gallon jug of sweet milk. By the time the stage reached Garnet after climbing the steep, log-lined grade that reminded Elizabeth of corduroy, it had jostled so much that there was always butter on top. Elizabeth returned to Garnet many years later and was shocked at how little of what she remembered was left in the town.

Mary Ann Combs

THE Bitterroot Salish left their beloved Bitterroot Valley for the Flathead Reservation in 1891. Salish elder Louis Adams retells the sad story as his ancestor Mary Ann Combs told it to him. Mary Ann, who died in 1977 at age ninety-eight, lived as a girl in the Bitterroot Valley. Her family farmed, and their white neighbors were good to them. Mary Ann remembered that the morning they left the Bitterroot was clear and lovely; she was twelve years old. U.S. Army troops gathered the several hundred Salish together and informed them that they were to move to the reservation immediately. Mary Ann was afraid as the soldiers marched her people out of the valley at gunpoint. During the several days' journey, the soldiers were disrespectful and warned the people not to leave the trail for any reason, even when the women and children needed to relieve themselves. It was degrading and humiliating. Everyone cried as they dragged their tipi poles behind their horses past the fences that divided off the land that had once been their homeland. But there is more to the story, as Louis Adams tells. When he was a little boy and his relatives gathered, adults whispered when the children were out of earshot. As soon as children entered the room, conversation would stop. When Louis was a teenager, he discovered why. His aunt explained to him that the family was very angry when the government forced them to leave their Bitterroot homeland. However, the family elders who participated in the departure did not want their children to carry on their broken hearts. "The reservation is your home, now," his aunt told him. "And you need to feel good about it." The elder family members kept their grief to themselves.

Camp Paxson Boy Scout Camp*

SEELEY LAKE is one link in a chain of five lakes nestled between the lofty Swan and Mission mountain ranges in western Montana. Two hundred acres of ancient larch trees surround the area, which has drawn visitors since the early 1900s. In 1924, the Forest Service granted a permit to the Western Montana Council of Boy Scouts to construct a summer camp in Missoula County. The facility was originally a tent camp, but by the late 1930s there was need for a more permanent facility. The Works Progress Administration (WPA) and Civilian Conservation Corps (CCC), New Deal programs vital to the nation's economic recovery during the depressed 1930s, provided funds and manpower to construct the present camp. The rustic log buildings were constructed in 1939–40 under the direction of Forest Service engineer Clyde Fickes. Camp Paxson is the only CCC-constructed youth camp in Montana. Designed to fit the natural landscape, the twenty buildings of saddle-notched native larch demonstrate excellent craftsmanship, remarkable since CCC workers were primarily "city boys" imported from urban areas back east who trained on the job. Several interior fireplaces of uncut native stone likewise reveal extraordinary masonry skills. Because of its public ownership and support, Camp Paxson has long provided recreational opportunities to diverse youth organizations. In 1995, the Missoula Children's Theatre secured a special use permit from the

Lolo National Forest to manage Camp Paxson. Named for Montana artist Edgar S. Paxson, the facility serves as a center for drama training, retreats, children's music camp, youth law enforcement camp, disadvantaged youth and other youth groups, and family reunions.

Muriel Murphy

FEW stories of women inmates at the Montana State Prison have happy endings. The story of the youngest person to receive a life sentence in Montana is an exception. In 1936, fifteen-year-old Muriel Murphy stood accused with her boyfriend, eighteen-year-old William Newman, of luring elderly Gust Anderson out of a Great Falls bar to steal his wallet. The prosecution maintained that Newman hit Anderson over the head and left him lying on the sidewalk. Anderson died of pneumonia two days later. Because the robbery resulted in a death, the charge was first-degree murder. The teens claimed Anderson had grabbed Muriel and Newman hit Anderson in defending her. The state waived the death penalty, leaving Judge H. H. Ewing no option but to sentence both to life in prison. Upon pronouncing sentence, the judge told the teens: "This sentence does not really mean what it says. Apply to the executive department when the time comes and I will do all I can." Both Muriel and William served three years and then left Deer Lodge on conditional pardons. The couple eventually married, left the state, and started a family. W. L. Fitzsimmons, clerk of the State Board of Examiners, corresponded with the Newmans as a condition of their release. After ten years, he wrote a final letter, informing them that they had fulfilled the conditions and that all rights of citizenship lost by reason of conviction were officially restored. In a rare expression of goodwill, Fitzsimmons wished the Newmans every success and assured them that he was not tracking them but hoped that they would stay in touch.

Educating and Correcting Youth

A Lesson on the Trail

MANY families traveled by wagon or by steamboat to Montana's goldfields in the mid-1860s. Some families had to cope with tragedies, but many families greatly enjoyed their journeys west. The Jonas Butts family left Independence, Missouri, wintered in Denver, and arrived at Virginia City, Montana, in the summer of 1864. Derinda Jane Butts was eight years old. She and her two sisters, Arminda Ellen and Sarah Anne, were not used to luxuries anyway, and were accustomed to making do with what little they had, so they did not miss creature comforts on the journey west. The family had no mishaps along the way, so Derinda Jane and her two sisters regarded the trip as a great adventure. They had a wonderful time riding in the wagon and camping out. But Derinda Jane had one very vivid recollection of a lesson that all of the children traveling with the train learned. The children had all been warned repeatedly about staying close to the wagons. One evening after the wagon train had made camp for the night, some of the children ran up a hill away from the encampment. When they reached the top of the hill, they saw the shadowy form of an Indian moving from bush to bush. The children were terrified. They ran all the way down the hill and back to camp, screaming and breathlessly describing the Indian they had seen stalking the camp. It turned out to be one of

87

the train's own men, stripped to the waist and covered in dark mud. It was his way of teaching the children the danger of wandering away from camp. After this experience, the children never strayed too far from their parents.

Indian Boarding Schools

RICHARD PRATT founded the first off-reservation Indian boarding school in the 1870s. Based on Pratt's philosophy to kill the Indian and save the child, these schools endured well beyond the mid-twentieth century. By 1885, there were sixty government-run boarding schools across the United States. By law all Indian children had to attend. Taken from their parents—sometimes by force—children as young as four traveled to distant schools where they stayed for nine years. Most of these schools were former military forts, not meant for little children. The aim was to civilize, Christianize, and "de-tribalize" all Indians. Franci Taylor's grandmother went as a young child from the Northern Cheyenne Reservation in eastern Montana to the Indian school in Carlisle, Pennsylvania. Upon arrival, the children's clothing and possessions—often items lovingly made by cherished family members—were burned in front of them. Officials bathed the children in sheep dip to rid them of parasites, gave them English names, dressed them in heavy wool uniforms and stiff boots and shoes, and cut their hair. Short hair was a sign of mourning, and children often thought their hair was cut because their parents had died. Sometimes parents did die, but the children did not know until they returned home years later. Students went through the third grade and no further; Franci's grandmother, for example, repeated the three grades three times in her nine years at school. Girls trained to be domestic servants, and boys learned farm labor. Very harsh punishments for minor offenses included beatings, scrubbing floors while kneeling on rice, and solitary confinement. While not all boarding school experiences were negative, the Kennedy Report in 1969 declared the Indian education system a national tragedy. Indian schools still exist today, but most are now under Native American administration.

Bannack School

THE Masonic Lodge* in the ghost town of Bannack was designed to serve a double function as a fraternal meeting hall and a schoolhouse. The odd combination was really not so strange. Masons were a strong presence in Montana Territory, and education of children on the frontier was one of the first considerations in the earliest mining camps. A double ceiling and floor between stories kept the ground-floor school and the upstairs meeting room entirely soundproof and separate to protect the Masons' secret rites. An outside stairway provided access to the meeting room. The final element the building required was a large, smooth piece of wood on which the lodge numbers and emblem could be carved. But Bannack had no piece of wood large enough or smooth enough for the purpose. Then a woman came forward and offered her treasured breadboard brought from her home back east. W. G. Blair carved the lodge numbers and the Masonic square and compass upon it. Workmen installed it beneath the peak of the roof. The Masons used the lodge hall only briefly, but the school long served Bannack's children. By the mid-twentieth century, however, the building sagged. Its roof disintegrated, the windows stood open to the elements, and only shreds of paint covered the outside walls. The carved breadboard, once tucked under the roof's peak, was removed for safekeeping. In 1954, Bannack became a state park, and in the 1970s, staff began preservation of the Masonic Lodge. Reinstalling the cherished breadboard to its original position was the final step, and there it remains today.

Montana State School*

Montana pledged its commitment to children with disabilities in 1887 when territorial governor Preston Leslie requested funds for a Montana Deaf and Dumb Asylum. Its title, although shocking by today's standards, reflects accepted nineteenth-century terminology and attitudes. Upon statehood in 1889, Congress granted Montana fifty thousand acres of land to raise funds for the school. The 1893 legislature provided operating expenses and chose Boulder as the site. Students attended classes in a private home until the school, begun in 1896, was completed in 1898. Despite its formidable name, the school offered innovative college-preparatory instruction and training for deaf and blind youth. In 1903, the state legislature changed the name to the Montana School for the Deaf and Dumb, thereby acknowledging that it was not an asylum, but rather a public school for children with special needs. By 1915, additional buildings increased the campus capacity to two hundred students, who ranged from ages five to twenty. By this time its mission had expanded to include educating developmentally disabled youth. Until the 1930s, the main building served numerous purposes as the center of activities, housing for students and staff, and dining rooms. In addition to the usual public school curriculum, blind students learned various manual industries and deaf students learned lip-reading. The school also offered an extensive music program. The original historic building, designed by state architect John C. Paulsen, is appropriately trimmed in Montana copper and sits at the edge of the more modern campus. Its institutional service recalls a state milestone.

Mountain View School for Girls*

The Montana legislature created the Boys and Girls Industrial School at Miles City in 1893. This reformatory was for boys and girls who were either in serious trouble with the law or had nowhere else to go. It was one step toward the establishment of the juvenile court system that came about in 1907. Some felt strongly that there should be separate industrial schools for boys and girls. One of these advocates was Dr. Maria Dean, a Helena physician whose practice specialized in the diseases of women and children. A great humanitarian, Dr. Dean took up many causes during her lifetime, but she felt most strongly about separating boys and girls in detention. Dr. Dean worked tirelessly with other women's groups toward this end, and finally, in 1919, legislator Emma Ingalls sponsored a bill establishing the Mountain View Vocational School for Girls in Helena. Dr. Dean died just weeks after the bill passed. The first six girls were transferred from Miles City to the new facility seven miles north of Helena in April 1920. By 1922, fifty-three girls between the ages of nine and eighteen lived in cottages on the campus. Some were orphans, some were runaways, and others had behavioral problems. Until the 1950s, harsh discipline included solitary confinement and lockup. By the 1960s, there was more emphasis on education and less on punishment. In 1996, the school closed and the Montana Law Enforcement Academy moved in. A few buildings, stables, and attic graffiti recall the former use of the campus.

Trask Hall*

ELEVEN years before statehood, Deer Lodge became home to Montana's first postsecondary school: the Montana Collegiate Institute. The nonsectarian, protestant, coeducational college offered both high school classes and a classical graduating course "as comprehensive and thorough as that of most seminaries and female colleges." Architects from Chicago designed the institute's first building. However, the building committee stripped the design of much of its ornamentation after it received the initial construction bids. The simplified two-story Trask Hall was constructed in 1878 for approximately thirteen thousand dollars using locally quarried granite and bricks imported from Helena. The school folded under financial strain after only a year. Three years later, the Presbyterian Church acquired the institute and changed its name to the College of Montana. Nationally, Presbyterians saw the college as part of their campaign to compete with Catholic institutions and civilize and Christianize the West. A generous East Coast donor, Alanson Trask, paid the school's remaining six-thousand-dollar debt. Trask Hall was then renamed in his honor. At its peak, the college boasted fifteen faculty and 160 students, housed in two dormitories. Among the faculty was Theodore Brantly, who became chief justice of the Montana Supreme Court upon statehood. The school closed in 1900, unable to compete with the new, state-funded university system. It reopened under different management in 1906 only to close for good in 1917. In 1921, School District One purchased the campus, including Trask Hall. Nevertheless, Montana's Presbyterians continued to support higher education, ultimately uniting with other denominations to found Rocky Mountain College in Billings.

Superior School Building*

TRAVELERS along the Mullan Road and prospectors lured by the 1869 discovery of gold on Cedar Creek opened the way for settlement of this area. After the placer gold played out and other mining camps became ghost towns, the town of Superior continued to grow. In 1891, the community organized a school district, and elementary classes were held in a small log cabin. By 1892, there were ninety school-age children in the vicinity. Into the 1900s, several rural schools accommodated local children, but none offered a high school curriculum. Older students had to leave home to advance beyond the primary grades. Mineral County was organized in 1914, and a year later bonds for the construction of a high school passed. The district offered a secondary curriculum for the first time that fall with classes held in the Methodist Church basement; students from all over the county attended. The new high school, constructed by local builder Charles Augustine at a cost of ten thousand dollars, was dedicated on January 28, 1916. Additions in 1925 and 1947 eased overcrowding, and the school remained in use until June 1995. It is today one of Montana's few examples of colonial revival–style school architecture. Along with the Mineral County Courthouse, this impressive landmark with its three-stage bell tower, flanking dormers, and strict classical symmetry has always drawn visitors to the center of town. Despite its closure, the Superior School maintains a strong visual presence at the heart of the community where for eighty years it served the county and its children.

Paris Gibson Junior High Blows Up

GREAT FALLS Central High School* opened in 1896. It took a creative community three years to build it. To prepare the uneven ground, sheepherders drove a herd of sheep around the site one hundred times trampling down the dirt. Huge logs floated to Great Falls on the Missouri River were shaved flat on all four sides and became the beams for the floor supports, attic framework, and stairways. The massive blocks of sandstone that form the walls came from a quarry near Helena and rest on a foundation sixteen feet thick in some places. Great Falls judged Central the best school west of the Mississippi. Its crowning feature, a huge Norman-style clock tower, arose out of the central part of the building. However, it was so heavy that it finally became unsafe, and the school took it down in 1916. According to locals, the custodian and his family lived in the school's attic. A sink with running water and wallpaper on the walls made the apartment quite homey. The daughter, however, was embarrassed to be living in the school's attic. She would leave home early in the morning, walk away from the building before the other students began to arrive, and then walk to school with her classmates. In 1913, a brick annex with an auditorium and gymnasium doubled the size of the school. From 1930 to the 1970s, the school served as Paris Gibson Junior High. In 1977, it became the Paris Gibson Square Museum of Art. But just before this adaptive reuse, moviemakers blew up the annex in a spectacular controlled demolition for a scene in *Telefon,* starring Charles Bronson and Lee Remick.

The M*

EVER wondered about letters on hillsides? Many Montana communities display these letters, often visible for miles on barren slopes. These familiar icons seem to be a product of the American West and a reminder that school was not all study. According to the experts, the University of California Berkeley boasts the first hillside letter, a giant C displayed in 1905. Other

University of Montana students perform the ritual painting of the M on Mount Sentinel, Missoula, 1957.

colleges and universities soon followed suit. As land-grant colleges became established in western states newly admitted to the Union, they joined the tradition. Montana has 112 hillside letters, more than any other state. The University of Montana's M, however, was the state's first. Carroll College in Helena, Montana State University in Bozeman, Montana Tech in Butte, and the University of Montana Western in Dillon all display hillside letters. Other smaller schools and high schools, inspired by Missoula's M, also joined the trend. Students constructed Missoula's first M of whitewashed rock in 1909. Throughout the early decades, upper classmen used the M to exert authority over the freshman who were responsible for its upkeep. The sophomore class replaced the first M with an upright wooden model outfitted with eighteen dollars' worth of lights. A larger wooden M soon replaced the upright one, but students did not properly attach the pieces and a blizzard carried them off. Forestry students built the trail leading up to the M in 1915. It has since served university and community groups that have used the M to advertise events or causes, and it has seen demonstrations and pranks. And once, with the addition of giant letters, a creative suitor even spelled out the message, "MARRY ME!" If the offer was accepted, it is not on record. Hillside letters like the M, regardless of one's alma mater, recall all those years each of us spent being educated.

What They Left Behind

Crow Agency Archaeology

ARCHEOLOGICAL investigations have recently exposed the foundations of the second Crow agency in the Stillwater Valley near Absarokee. A full-scale excavation, conducted by Aaberg Cultural Resources, came about as preliminary to the Montana Department of Transportation's planned widening of a three-mile stretch of Highway 78. Testing for archaeological sites is required for projects that disturb the right-of-way. The highway bisected the suspected location of the agency that existed there between 1875 and 1884. The agency is historically important because it encompasses a difficult period in Crow history. Not only were the Crows struggling to transition from hunting to farming during this decade, the tribe also suffered from epidemics of measles and scarlet fever. Preliminary test pits of the area yielded enough artifacts to warrant further investigation. In 2006, Steve Aaberg surveyed the site with a magnetometer. This instrument reveals solid objects underground and translates them to a computer-generated map. Comparing his findings with an 1878 map of the agency, Aaberg determined that the rectangular compound exactly lined up with scattered anomalies the magnetometer revealed. This exciting discovery led to the excavations in the summer of 2011. Crews uncovered portions of the foundations of the compound that included the agent's, clerk's, and doctor's offices. A layer of charcoal and ash substantiates the fact that the site was burned upon abandonment. Decorative beads, animal bones, broken bottles, and other artifacts, currently under analysis, will eventually be housed at the curation facility on the Little Big Horn College campus in Crow Agency. Study of these artifacts and the tragic story they tell will help write this chapter of Montana's past.

Medicine Rocks State Park

One of Montana's most spectacular places is the 320-acre Medicine Rocks State Park in Carter County. These great sandstone pillars are the result of eons of wind, which still blows relentlessly across the prairie. Eastern Montana once marked the shore of an ancient inland sea that covered most of the state. Some geologists theorize that the Medicine Rocks were once sand dunes. Today, the wind's unearthly song sighs through the odd openings in the rocks. The Arikaras, Assiniboines, Mandans, Gros Ventres, Sioux, and Cheyennes all traveled through and camped among these hauntingly beautiful formations. The Sioux called the columns with Swiss cheese–like openings *Inyan-oka-la-ka*, which means "Rock with a hole in it." It was a sacred place where, according to one Sioux, "the spirits stayed and the medicine men prayed." The magical place saw generations of hunting parties and medicine men conjuring spirits. Tipi rings, stone tools, bone artifacts, and shards of primitive pottery are evidence that native peoples frequented the area. A freshwater spring added to the attraction, and later, cattle drives and settlers moved through. Medicine Rocks was one of Montana's first tourist attractions. Young Teddy Roosevelt was an early visitor who described the park "as fantastically beautiful a place" as he had ever seen. Carter County gained title when the owners defaulted on taxes during the Great Depression in the 1930s. In 1957, the county gave the park to the State of Montana and its Fish and Wildlife division began to manage it as a natural reserve in 1965. If you visit this special place, stay until sundown and listen carefully. You can hear the primeval flutelike voices still singing their ancient song.

Remnants of Native Culture in Southwestern Montana

THERE is history and tradition around every corner in southwestern Montana. Visual reminders of rich Indian culture and tribal journeys are obvious if you know what to look for. By the end of the last Ice Age, North America's first people lived and traveled in the Helena valley in what is now Lewis and Clark County, stopping at the MacHaffie Site* near Montana City to quarry chert for weapons and tools. Stone quarry sites like Mammoth Meadows in Beaverhead County and the Cashman Quarry in Madison County recall an industry essential to survival. Broadwater County's abundant tipi rings—amazingly clear in aerial photographs—served generations of travelers. Native people considered the Boulder Hot Springs* in Jefferson County such an important place that they called it Peace Valley, and it was a place of truce. The Warm Springs Mound* in the Deer Lodge Valley, like a giant tipi with smoke curling out its top, served as a beacon to tribal groups and later to Métis Johnny Grant. As the founder of Powell County's Grant-Kohrs Ranch* (a National Historic Site), Grant and his multicultural family were the first permanent settlers in the Deer Lodge Valley. Beaverhead Rock in Beaverhead County guided Sacajawea and generations of her people. Her Shoshone kin and countless others traveled over treacherous Lemhi Pass*, a National Historic Landmark, to hunt buffalo. The serenity of the beautiful Big Hole National Battlefield* belies the terrible clash that cost the lives of Nez Perce men, women, and children. The relocation of urban Crees to Butte* in the late nineteenth and early twentieth centuries recalls the more recent struggles of Indian people. Scattered tipi rings, buffalo kills, pictographs, quarry sites, remnants of the Old North Trail, and other resources remind the visitor that Indian roots are firmly planted in this part of Montana.

A Curiosity

J. L. CAMPBELL'S travel guide to the Territory of Idaho, published in 1864, was intended to aid would-be emigrants contemplating a journey to the new goldfields. Campbell traveled the region in 1863, but by 1864, when his guide, *Idaho: Six Months in the New Gold Regions,* was published, it was already outdated. Montana Territory had been carved out of the vast chunk of Idaho. Campbell's guide, however, was a useful tool describing the route from Omaha, Nebraska, to the diggings at Bannack and Virginia City. Campbell offers advice, suggests items to take on the journey, and lists good campsites. His description of the Bannack mines includes a fascinating historical tidbit. He claims that he saw an ancient mine shaft where the miners presumably dug down to gold. A large pine tree, one foot in diameter, had grown in the mine shaft, attesting to the age of the mine. A couple of ancient timber huts stood nearby. Campbell noted that in the dry climate, timber exposed to weather could last a very long time. He theorized that the mines were the work of Spaniards who came north from Mexico exploring in the 1700s as some chronicles suggest. Most modern historians agree, however, that Spanish explorers did not venture this far north. A more likely explanation for this anomaly is that the mine was a stone quarry where Native Americans dug for chert to make weapons. Certainly the timber huts are Native American wickiups, not shelters of Spanish origin. These temporary shelters do survive to great age and—along with tipi rings, rock cairns, and other manmade features—are part of Montana's archaeological record.

Chinese in Big Timber

THE story of Montana's Chinese pioneers has almost entirely escaped the state's written history. By 1870, Chinese comprised 10 percent of Montana's population, but by the mid-1950s, few remained. Their homes and businesses fell victim to urban renewal programs. Time erased their remote mining and railroad camps. Traces of their culture disappeared, and their stories have become the stuff of myth and legend. In 2008, Big Timber gave up some information about its Chinese residents. University of Montana archaeology students uncovered a Chinese restaurant and laundry next to a brothel. Historic maps confirm that Chinese businesses and a female boardinghouse—the euphemism for prostitution—operated in the neighborhood in the early 1900s. Western red-light districts and Chinese settlements, both housing outcast populations, were often adjacent. Volunteers working on the Big Timber project unearthed thirty-five thousand artifacts, which comprise Montana's only known Chinese deposit of the 1930s and 1940s. Among the artifacts are shards of pottery and porcelain, a bluing ball used in laundry operations, Chinese game pieces, and one very curious item. Intentionally placed beneath the doorframe of the entryway was a domestic cat's paw. Likely some kind of talisman, its placement remains a mystery. The crew also accessed Big Timber's tunnels, which locals insist are Chinese. But in Big Timber, as in other communities, passageways dubbed "Chinese tunnels" are nothing more than convenient access or under-sidewalk storage.

Poacher Gulch

TALES of Chinese terraces along a heavily timbered hillside in Sanders County attracted the attention of Forest Service and University of Montana archaeologists in 2006. The site was unlike any other in Montana. The rock-lined terraces, moss-covered with age, spanned several hundred feet cut into a steep slope. Forest Service archaeologists had discovered these terraces in 1979 tucked away in an obscure drainage known as Poacher Gulch. Locals firmly believed that Chinese miners built them. As the story went, Chinese workers laying tracks of the Northern Pacific Railroad along the Clark Fork River in 1883, underpaid and mistreated, left their jobs to search the hills for gold and silver. It was logical, and these terraces resembled terraces Chinese farmers constructed in Idaho's Payette National Forest. So between 1979 and 2006, the Chinese terrace theory was so convincing that it nearly became accepted as fact. Archaeologists assumed they would discover evidence of Chinese occupation during the 1880s when laborers were laying track along the Clark Fork River. To their great surprise, however, they found no evidence of Chinese. Instead, they found the cultivation of corn on the terraces, thousands of tiny pieces of tarpaper, mushy wood, and nails dating to the early 1900s. The Chinese terraces of Poacher Gulch turned out to be something completely unexpected. No Chinese ever lived there. Its real inhabitants cultivated corn for moonshine.

Chinese Settlements

In the 1990s, Forest Service archaeologists excavated several sites occupied by Chinese miners during the nineteenth century. At China Gulch near Superior in western Montana's Mineral County, archaeologists found curious U-shaped, hand-stacked rock hearths and mysterious small metal trays they called "thingies." The University of Idaho's Asian expert, Dr. Priscilla Wegars, eventually identified the thingies as funs trays, modified opium cans used to weigh and measure the drug. Recent excavations of Chinese hearths at nearby Cedar Creek yielded clues about the poor quality of life in this remote mining camp where three hundred Chinese miners spent the winter in 1870. Analysis of pig, deer, and sheep bone fragments found in the hearths revealed that they had been cooked at least four different times. This tells a sad story: the people living there were starving and making do with very little. The hearths found here and elsewhere in Montana are unique to the Chinese. They differ from Italian or Slavic bread ovens, which are often mistakenly called Chinese ovens. The Chinese did not make bread. Another site, German Gulch near Butte, excavated in the 1980s, yielded many artifacts that were not studied until the early 2000s. The German Gulch artifacts form the best collection of Chinese materials found in Montana to date. Items include such imported foodstuffs as Chinese dates and olives, sheephead fish, and flounder, illustrating a sophisticated trade network. One curious feature at the site is a type of kiln, possibly a crematorium. While there is no physical evidence of human cremation, the *New Northwest* magazine noted in 1874 the cremation of six Chinese at German Gulch.

Pictograph Cave Cannibals

ENGLISH professor H. Melville Sayre of the Montana School of Mines at Butte led the first archaeological excavations at Pictograph Cave*, a National Historic Landmark, near Billings. Under foreman Oscar T. Lewis, a Glendive rancher and self-taught archaeologist, the dig was funded by the Depression-era New Deal Works Progress Administration of the 1930s. It put numerous crew members to work. According to locals who frequented the excavation site as visitors in 1937 and 1938, both Sayre and Lewis told fantastic tales. They claimed to have found evidence that Ice Age occupants practiced cannibalism. They backed up their story with the supposed discovery of human teeth, a human skull with knife marks consistent with removal of the tongue, and butchered human rib bones bearing human teeth marks. While Sayre's formal report to Governor Roy Ayers is considerably less flamboyant, he does

Montana Historical Society Photograph Archives, Helena, PAc 84-91 A 7910-7

Pictograph Cave, Pictograph Cave State Park, near Billings

mention that some items yielded evidence consistent with cannibalistic activity. Lewis further speculates in his notes that notched bone projectile points found in the caves came from Inuits in the Arctic. He figured that the Inuits harpooned buffalo that did not die but migrated south, where they were eventually killed by the early inhabitants of the Yellowstone Valley. Writer Glendolin Damon Wagner, who wrote about evidence of cannibalism among other indigenous peoples, painted a vivid picture of the finds in Pictograph Cave in the *Rocky Mountain Husbandman* of May 3, 1938. But when professional archaeologist Dr. William Mulloy took over the Pictograph Cave excavations in 1941, these tales died a swift death. If evidence of cannibalism existed, it has been lost along with many of the artifacts discovered under Lewis and Sayre. Most scientists discount cannibalism among Montana's first peoples as nothing more than bunk.

Trail of Destruction

BEFORE whites settled in eastern Montana, Irish nobleman Sir George Gore enjoyed a hunting trip of astonishing destruction. An Oxford-educated scholar and avid hunter, Sir George had thrilled to tales of the American West and organized a three-year hunting trip. His party set out from Westport, Missouri, in 1854 under sanction of the American Fur Trading Company. Famed mountain man Jim Bridger guided the caravan, which included 110 horses, twenty yoke of oxen, fifty hunting hounds, and twenty-eight vehicles, sixteen of them carrying Sir George's luggage. When the party camped, a large green and white striped canvas wall tent provided Sir George's shelter. French carpet, heating stoves, a brass bedstead, a steel bathtub, an oak dining set, and a commode with a fur-lined seat and removable pot promised Sir George all the comforts. For two years he passed the evenings enjoying sumptuous banquets, fine wine, and literary discussions with Bridger. By day on his gray thoroughbred named Steel Trap, Sir George pursued game. Aside from trophy heads, he rarely retrieved the meat, leaving it to spoil. After Sir George devastated the Yellowstone Valley in 1856, Crow estimates of his terrible waste there included 105 bears, more than two thousand bison, and 1,600 elk and deer. His reputation preceded him, however. In the Black Hills en route to St. Louis, his party fell prey to a band of Sioux. Stripped naked and forced to abandon their goods, the arrogant slob hunter and his party experienced survival for real. During his stay in Montana, Sir George left one lasting legacy. He named the Yellowstone's local tributary "Glendive," from which the town, some twenty-five years later, took its name.

The Verendryes

PIERRE GAULTIER DE VARENNES, Sieur de la Verendrye, started out from Montreal in 1831 to find the Sea of the West or the mythical Northwest Passage. Discovery of this supposed waterway to the Pacific would assure the discoverer a monopoly in the trade with China. From the Indians, Verendrye learned of the mountains of shining stones and a great salt lake that he took to be the Pacific Ocean. On his travels Verendrye saw the shining mountains—what we today call the Rocky Mountains—and traveled as far south as the Missouri River. But jealous rivalries and mounting debts forced him to return to France. Twelve years later, Verendrye's sons Francois and Louis Joseph continued their father's quest to find the Northwest Passage. Their route is not documented, but they likely traveled into what is now southeastern Montana. Thus the Verendryes were the first white explorers to set foot in the state, and the journals describing their explorations are the first written descriptions of the Northwest. Even though they traveled farther into the American heartland than any other European explorers, their contemporaries dismissed them as failures since they did not find the Northwest Passage. In March 1743, the brothers stood on a hill overlooking the place where Pierre, South Dakota, would one day be built. There they buried a lead plate claiming the lands of the entire Missouri River drainage for France. The plate was discovered 170 years later in 1913 by children playing on the hill. They tried to sell it to the local tinsmith. Historian Doane Robinson fortunately intercepted the sale and saved the plate. The site, Verendrye Hill* in South Dakota, is a National Historic Landmark.

Bear Paw Trail

BEAVER CREEK PARK in Hill County near Havre is the nation's largest county park. It is also one of few parks that integrates annual haying and livestock grazing to generate funds and reduce fire danger. The Hill County Conservation District developed the Bear Paw Nature Trail in 2005. The three-mile trail offers a fascinating hike along a road built by soldiers at nearby Fort Assinniboine*.

Charged with patrolling the international border, the fort sheltered eight hundred officers and enlisted men, several hundred family members, and nonmilitary employees. It was Montana's largest military fort. Soldiers garrisoned there never saw direct action, but the men trained rigorously and were ready for service at a moment's notice. The road along Beaver Creek provided access to the summer encampment at Dillons Bottom and to areas used to practice maneuvers. It also provided a route to the timberlands in the upper reaches of the Bears Paw Mountains. The fort employed many seasonal woodcutters. Cordwood was crucial for cooking and for heating the fort's buildings. Laborers cut and stacked the wood. Then, in the spring when the water was high, they returned to float the wood down Beaver Creek and haul it along the road to the fort. According to early sources, there were no fish in Beaver Creek when the first soldiers arrived in 1879. They transported fish in canvas buckets from Birch Creek and dumped them in upper Beaver Creek, where the population thrived. Thereafter, fishing in Beaver Creek provided sport for the men and fresh fish for the table. The road thus served recreational purposes historically just as it does today.

Montana's First Condo

BACK in 1977, the Montana Ghost Town Preservation Society published a small booklet entitled *If These Walls Could Talk*. It includes the first published walking tour of Virginia City. The authors, including longtime Virginia City advocate John Ellingsen, tell a curious tale about the vacant lot just east of the Fairweather Inn*. On this lot in 1865, grocer E. Olinghouse built a very fine stone building. It was the best, most substantial office building in the territory at that time. Over the years various businesses— including the post office—operated in the Olinghouse Block, and for a brief time the second floor even housed the district court. In 1876, Patrick Largey of Butte—sometimes known as the fourth copper king—bought the second floor, making it unofficially Montana's first condo. Virginia City banker Henry Elling eventually held title to the first floor, and by 1900 there was an assay office in the basement. In 1910, an explosion in the assay office blew out the foundation's east wall, and the building collapsed on itself. Remnant walls of the beautiful stone Olinghouse Block were pulled down and the debris hauled away. The Largey estate continued to pay taxes on the nonexistent second floor until 1930 when the city acquired the title for $2.59. It was hardly worth even that with the first floor missing. Today, every trace of the building has disappeared. Well, almost. Archaeologists recently excavating in the empty parking lot discovered the charred remains of the basement.

The Good, the Bad, and Otherwise

Reed and Bowles

THE Reed and Bowles Trading Post* outside Lewistown is a little-known gem well worth a visit. The oldest standing building in the area, the post originally stood about a mile and a half southeast of its present location. It was part of a short-lived post called Fort Sherman intended to serve a large Crow reservation, but by 1874 the plans for the reservation had fallen through. Construction of the Carroll Trail, a freighting route between Carroll on the Missouri River and Helena, prompted Alonzo S. Reed and John Bowles—a notorious pair—to purchase the post, dismantle it, and move it to its present site along Spring Creek. The post served traffic along the trail between 1875 and 1880 and catered to the many tribes passing through. Major Reed—so called from his brief stint as Milk River Indian agent, from which he was fired—was the kingpin and Bowles was his assistant. Reed reputedly settled disputes with gunfire and planted his victims in the burial ground across the river. Bowles supposedly even sold the bones of his father-in-law, the Crow leader Long Horse, to an Irish ornithologist. The pair was well known for brutality toward their wives, drunken sprees, and trading liquor with the Indians, a violation of federal law. Reed and Bowles sold a wicked brew of ethanol laced with plug tobacco and red pepper. During the five years the post operated, visitors included

American naturalist George Bird Grinnell, trader Pike Landusky, "Liver Eating" Johnson, and the Nez Perces, who stopped there briefly to rest in 1877 during their tragic flight from the U.S. Army.

Henry Plummer

HENRY PLUMMER, the onetime sheriff of Bannack hanged by the vigilantes, is a controversial figure whose actions have been hotly debated. Was he a good guy wrongly accused, or was he guilty of highway robberies and murders? Setting that issue aside, however, a look at Plummer's activities in Nevada City, California, provides interesting insight. Plummer was serving as town marshal when he shot and killed Henry Vedder over the affections of Vedder's wife. Apologists claim that Plummer only wanted to help Vedder's abused wife get away. Plummer was convicted of murder, but charges of jury misconduct resulted in a mistrial. Plummer was tried again, and again found guilty. Sentenced to ten years at San Quentin, Plummer used his considerable charm and good connections to convince prison officials that he was terminally ill with tuberculosis. Official prison correspondence reveals that Plummer asked for a pardon, not claiming innocence, but because he had only months to live and wanted to die at home. Plummer's well-connected friends also wrote letters to Governor John B. Weller to that effect. The governor, moved by Plummer's illness, issued a full pardon. After serving only six months of his sentence, Plummer returned to Nevada City and was soon so healthy that the town reinstated him as marshal. Plummer was then involved in two more killings in Nevada City. Arrested in the second, he escaped from the jail and fled to Oregon. The editor of the local Nevada City newspaper noted Plummer's hasty retreat: "Good Riddance of a sinister, dangerous man." Plummer clearly carried plenty of baggage. Whether guilty or innocent of crimes in Montana, the controversy he continues to stir proves that history is not dead.

Crow leader Plenty Coups, June 7, 1921

Plenty Coups

ALEEK-CHEA-AHOOSH, or Many Achievements, was a fitting name for the influential Crow chief who was esteemed among his people and honored by both statesmen and presidents. White men called him Plenty Coups for the eighty feathers he wore with earned authority on his coup stick. A veteran warrior and shrewd negotiator, Plenty Coups was also a true, if sometimes critical, patriot and friend to the white man. At the age of ten, Plenty Coups had a dream that foretold the demise of the buffalo. His tribe realized the poignant truth of this vision, and unlike others, the Crows resignedly "pointed their guns with the white man's." The passing of the buffalo brought irreparable change, and Plenty Coups served as a bridge for his people between the old ways and the new. On the reservation he learned to farm and in 1888 chose a place to build a home of square-hewn logs; in keeping with native custom, the door faces east. Completed in 1906, it was the reservation's only two-story building. Plenty Coups and his wife, Strikes-the-Iron, executed a Deed of Trust providing that forty acres of the farm be "set aside as a park and recreation ground for members of the Crow Tribe of Indians and white people jointly." The government symbolically accepted this gift at a great ceremony in 1928. Plenty Coups died in 1932 at the age of eighty-four. He was the last chief of the Crow Nation, so venerated that his people never named a successor. The designation of Chief Plenty Coups Memorial State Park* in 1965 would have been in accordance with his wishes. The site is now a National Historic Landmark.

Florence Clark

ANACONDA'S red-light district and its fancy women never equaled Butte's, but Florence Clark was one longtime flamboyant madam whose wealth and reputation came close. Her place of business in Anaconda was called the Monogram. Florence was often seen driving her expensive rubber-tired buggy on the city streets. She owned some famous racehorses, too. One of them, Silk Stocking, held a record and raced the circuits in Salt Lake City, Oakland, and Spokane. Although Florence had what money could buy, in 1905 she narrowly survived a well-publicized attempted suicide. She generously patronized local merchants; however, she was neither generous nor kind toward her female employees. In 1908, an Anaconda policeman heard that one of the Monogram's working girls wished to leave but was being held against her will. The investigating officer found a seventeen-year-old girl at the house and attempted to escort her out. Florence grabbed the girl to prevent her leaving. The officer had no choice but to punch Florence and knocked her unconscious. Several years later, in 1911, two women escaped from the Monogram and told authorities that Florence had kept them captive, taken their street clothes, charged exorbitant prices for their needs, and quickly made them deeply indebted to management. The women had worked for two years, their debts mounting every month. When the officer went to the Monogram to retrieve the women's belongings, he found their story to be true. The windows had steel bars like a jail. Life at the Monogram was nothing more than a life of bondage. Florence Clark's treatment of these women illustrates what some women truly experienced working for a madam.

Kirby Grant

HERE's a bit of Montana trivia. Kirby Grant Hoon Jr., who used the stage name Kirby Grant, starred in the 1950s television series *Sky King*. Remember that? He was born in Butte in 1911 and grew up in Helena, where his father, Kirby Grant Hoon Sr., was postmaster. Kirby Jr. was a 1929 graduate of Helena High School. In the series, he played wealthy Arizona rancher Schuyler King, nicknamed "Sky," who fought bad guys and rescued people with his airplane. His niece Penny, who lived with him on the Flying Crown Ranch, was his sidekick on these adventures. Kirby was a pilot in real life and learned to fly the airplanes in the series. Early television demanded simultaneous filming of multiple episodes, and so Sky wore the same clothes on every show. File footage, especially of the plane flying, was often used numerous times, and sometimes the film would be reversed so that the plane appeared to fly in the opposite direction. On these occasions, observant fans could notice that the numbers on the aircraft would be backward. Seventy-two episodes aired on ABC in 1953 and 1954. CBS later rebroadcast the series. Kirby Grant did little acting after *Sky King*. He and his wife founded a ranch for orphaned or abandoned children, and he was often honored at aviation events. On October 30, 1985, Kirby died in a traffic accident in Florida en route to the last successful launching of the space shuttle *Challenger*. Astronauts had planned to honor the Montana native for his encouragement of aviation and space flight.

Olive Warren

For seventy-five years, a concrete block inscribed with the name Olive Warren sat on Minnesota Avenue between Twenty-fifth and Twenty-sixth streets in Billings. Who was she? Legend says she arrived in the Magic City in 1897 from a convent in Denver. She beguiled a Billings attorney, and some say she cast her own magic spell on him. He showered her with jewelry, fancy clothes, and high-stepping horses. She cut a flamboyant figure, riding side-saddle on the streets of Billings. He gave her a huge diamond, and Olive named her establishment the Lucky Diamond after his gift. It was one of Montana's most elegant bordellos. The concrete block—a carriage step—kept gentlemen's feet out of the mud and ladies' slippers dry as they alighted from their horse-drawn conveyances at the Lucky Diamond. But all things fade, and Olive's business did too. She moved her girls elsewhere, and with federal closures of such places in 1917, Olive could no longer operate as openly. So she married James McDaniels, tried her luck ranching, divorced in 1932, and returned to Billings to run the Virginia Hotel. Her beauty dimmed. Olive Warren McDaniels died in 1943 of a kidney ailment. As she lay in her casket, dressed in a faded taffeta gown, the carriage stepping stone sat in front of a vacant lot. A Montana Power station was built where the Lucky Diamond stood, and the sidewalk was replaced. In 1972, Billings art enthusiast Harold Ruth took the step and placed it in the parking lot at his Gallery '85 on Emerald Drive. And there it remains today.

Vindex Family's Hard Times

WAY up in the northeast corner of the state, Plentywood experienced the worst of the Great Depression. Charles Vindex wrote about his family's experiences. In October 1929, an ice storm ended his road construction job; he did not work again until 1934. The landlord evicted the family from their rental in town. Charles, with his wife and newborn daughter, found an abandoned house seven miles out of town. He banked the crumbling foundation with manure and covered the broken windows with waterproof fabric. The wind howled endlessly, and the terrible dust even came up through the floorboards. Charles raised chickens and traded eggs for groceries. To keep their house warm, Charles hiked several miles twice daily to cut coal from a small vein, carrying the big chunks home in a sack on his back and smaller pieces in a bucket. A neighbor's cow supplied milk for the baby, but Charles had to hike a mile each way every day to milk her. In the summers, drought, swarms of locusts, cutworms, and army worms destroyed their garden again and again. Even the patches on their clothing had patches. Anticipating the birth of their second child, Charles got his wife to the Plentywood hospital in a borrowed car. By the time he returned the car and hiked seven miles back to the hospital, their son was several hours old. In a story published in *Montana The Magazine of Western History* in 1978, Charles Vindex wrote eloquently that if hard times like that ever return, his family learned how to get along and next time would do even better.

Gordon Family

JOHN GORDON was born in Scotland a free person of color. A trained chef, he came to Montana in 1881 to cook for the mining camps. John and his wife, Mary, settled in White Sulphur Springs, where John was chef at the Sherman Hotel. In 1895, Mary was pregnant with their fifth child when John left to take a job as chef for a Canadian railway. Soon after, he was killed in a train accident. Mary took in laundry, worked as a practical nurse, and cooked fine dinner parties for the town's elite. Her beautifully set tables sometimes baffled uneducated dinner guests. They would ask Mrs. Gordon what to do, and she would tell them to watch and do what the host did. She loved to tell how one old miner at a fancy banquet drank from his finger bowl. Mary's daughter Rose wanted to be a doctor. She had the aptitude but not the finances and instead became a physical therapist and practical nurse. Rose also owned a café and cooked fabulous meals. Taylor, the youngest child, led a charmed but tragic life. He was chauffeur for the president of the New York Metropolitan Opera, traveled with John Ringling's circus, and toured Europe with a gospel group. Taylor was a fine singer, performed on Broadway, and earned a place in Harlem's Renaissance of the 1920s. He also published an autobiography, *Born to Be*. But in 1947, a mental breakdown resulted in twelve years' hospitalization. Returning home, Taylor lived quietly and died in 1971. While the Gordons were a minority in White Sulphur Springs, Taylor wrote that he never saw prejudice in the place he called home.

Helena's Paul Revere

HELENA suffered numerous serious fires in the early years. Merchants sometimes had to rebuild their businesses more than once. Jacob Feldberg lost his clothing store to the fire of 1869 and understood the devastation it could cause. In 1871, another fire threatened Main Street. Jacob ran to help the firemen. "Go away, Jacob, and leave us alone," they told him. "You are too small to be of any help." Jacob was a man of very small stature, but he did not give up. He looked around to see what he could do. Wind was whipping through the gulch, and he saw burning embers flying up Broadway. Jacob yelled at the onlookers to follow him, and they ran up the street as firebrands struck their backs and sizzled at their feet. There were few houses except for a row in the first block of Fifth Avenue behind the courthouse. The neighborhood men were all away fighting the fire on Main Street, and Jacob found women and children madly throwing buckets of water on their homes. Jacob and his followers led horses to safety and turned out the cows, pigs, and chickens to fend for themselves. They thought the fire was nearly under control when a burning ember flew into a woodpile, which burst into flames. Jacob leapt upon a barn roof just as it collapsed and found his way into a kitchen. He gathered all the pots he could find, organized a bucket brigade, and saved the neighborhood. Ever after that, Jacob Feldberg was a hero, and for spreading the word of the fire, he earned the nickname "Helena's Paul Revere."

Daddy Reeves

A. I. "DADDY" REEVES came to Helena in 1892 and became a Christmas institution. The Reeves Music House brought many fine musicians and musical events to Helena. Reeves liked to tell the story about how he got his name. His parents weren't much on naming their large brood of children, and when he went to school, the only name he had was Baby. The teacher suggested he needed a name, so he came up with initials he chose from the alphabet the teacher had hung on the wall. The A and I don't stand for anything. In 1928, Reeves's business and a huge collection of sheet music went up in smoke when lightning struck a rooftop and burned nearly an entire city block. Reeves did not lament. He started again and ran his shop until he retired in about 1945 and moved to the Masonic home in the Helena Valley. Reeves, known to hundreds of kids as Daddy, taught music lessons to hundreds of Helena youths. He organized Helena's newsboys and the kids at Montana Deaconess School and St. Joseph's Orphanage into choirs and harmonica bands. Most children did not suspect that for more than fifty years Daddy Reeves was the official Elks Lodge Santa Claus. He never duplicated his grand entrances. He arrived by steam automobile or horse-drawn sleigh and once hid for hours in a fireplace

L. H. Jorud, photographer, Intermountain

Volunteer A. I. "Daddy" Reeves (left), of Reeves Music House; the harmonica choir of the Montana Deaconess School, Helena; and principal Helen C. Piper (right) in 1929

at the Montana Club before bursting out. In 1944, when Reeves played Santa for the fiftieth time at age eighty-two, the *Helena Independent* wished him the same amount of happiness to carry him over the trail of love, kindness, and joy he had blazed for Helena boys and girls.

Oscar Lewis

THE fabulous paintings on the walls of Pictograph Cave National Historic Landmark near Billings were long known to both Indians and locals. But in 1936, Glendive rancher Oscar T. Lewis discovered bone fragments and projectile points in the cave. Teaming up with H. Melville Sayre, an English professor at the Butte School of Mines, the two launched the first archaeological excavations at the cave. The New Deal Works Progress Administration funded and staffed this groundbreaking work. But as was common for the time, neither Sayre nor Lewis had formal archaeological training. Lewis headed the excavations. He was a flamboyant, self-taught character and a real legend in his own time. Born in a covered wagon in Wisconsin in 1887, at two he rode a horse to North Dakota with his mother, and at nine he made his own lead balls for a muzzle-loading shotgun and hunted game to feed his family of fourteen. He hunted wolves for bounty, posed for Charlie Russell's *Roping a Coyote,* and made some important archaeological discoveries, including the Hagan Site*, now a National Historic Landmark near Glendive. When Sayre died in 1941, respected University of Wyoming anthropologist Dr. William Mulloy took over the Pictograph Cave excavations. Mulloy made the site one of the most important of the northern plains. Although Lewis deserves credit as the first to recognize the cave's importance, Mulloy's classification of its thirty thousand artifacts—most of them unearthed under Lewis's supervision—became an archaeological benchmark. Mulloy respected Lewis's work, but the respect was understandably not mutual. When Lewis died in 1963, Mulloy said that Oscar was "one of the toughest old pieces of rawhide" he had ever known.

Mother Berry

ONE of Montana's most colorful characters was a woman known as Mother Berry. Her real name was Elizabeth Williams Berry, but Mother suited her just fine. Born in Australia in 1854, the feisty Elizabeth began a long career racing horses at age six. She became a jockey of great renown, racing all over the world under the name Jack Williams. Women jockeys were rare back then, and she disguised herself by wearing racing silks and a derby hat and smoking cigars. At the age of fifty-four, Elizabeth married veterinarian Dr. J. B. Berry, and they eventually moved to Helena. Here Dr. Berry had charge of the Kessler Brewery horses and the show stock of wealthy Yellowstone Park concessionaire Harry Child. After Dr. Berry died in 1927, Mother continued to own racehorses and made her home in a cottage near the fairgrounds at the back of the Lewis and Clark County Racetrack*. In 1937, fire claimed her home and the last of the oldest stables built before 1900. Her own prized Thoroughbred, Rosa Lockwood, was saved from the fire as were ten other valuable racehorses. Mother once told a reporter that she didn't like to have women around her because she feared she would say something bad. She learned to cuss from the jockeys she hung around with, and she was good at it too. When she turned one hundred, Mother said, "I'm not fit for the chopping block yet." She wasn't. When Mother turned 113, she was still doing all her own housework and cooking. She died in 1969, a month short of her 115th birthday.

Jean Baptiste Laurin

THE tiny town of Laurin in Madison County takes its name from wealthy French Canadian John Baptiste Laurin. The town, originally called Cicero, sprang up around John Baptiste's trading post and then became Laurin in 1874 after its founder. Jean Baptiste owned a great deal of local real estate—including toll bridges, ranches, and mining claims—within a wide radius. Revenue from his Big Hole Bridge alone totaled eight thousand dollars annually. Even though Jean Baptiste was completely illiterate and signed documents with a large, impressive X, he was a shrewd businessman. In 1865 he learned of Adaline Booth, whose husband had died in a shooting accident. Adaline was raising her sister's three children at nearby Adobetown and taking in laundry. Jean Baptiste sought her out, proposed, and married her. He was forty-four and she twenty-eight. They suited each other. Jean Baptiste, short and over 250 pounds, looked like an eight-gallon keg of beer, and Adaline was just as stout. The couple had a custom-made buggy with a heavy-duty suspension to hold their weight. Their fifteen-room home, still standing at Laurin, was a center of elegant hospitality. Full-length mirrors, a leather settee, and a huge sideboard freighted from St. Louis by steamboat and ox team were rare luxuries. Jean Baptiste was a money lender, charging up to 36 percent interest. When he died in 1896, locals claim that Adaline reduced borrowers' interest and never pressed them for payment. Adaline died a year later and left eight thousand dollars for the building of Laurin's quaint Catholic Church*. The couple had no children, but Jean Baptiste put two of Adaline's nephews through college.

Prison Escape

WARDEN FRANK CONLEY at the Montana State Prison in Deer Lodge kept fearsome full-blooded hounds trained to track escapees. They were enclosed in a high fence inside the prison walls. In 1902, prisoner Thomas O'Brien foiled these hounds in a spectacular getaway. O'Brien, who claimed he was innocent of grand larceny, had served half of his five-year sentence. He was a trustworthy prisoner who had some freedom in his assigned job as stable boss of the large barn outside the prison walls. O'Brien claimed he had veterinary training, and so he obtained medicines for the animals. He had worked for two weeks conditioning George Tighe, the warden's prize Thoroughbred racehorse. When the time was right, O'Brien obtained some opium, supposedly to treat one of the animals, and used it to put Warden Conley's bloodhounds into a deep slumber. He then calmly saddled George and rode off toward the prison ranches. The guards assumed that he was on some legitimate errand. As the distance between them grew greater, O'Brien coaxed the horse into his fastest run and went the other way. The hounds were of no use. Officials later found the saddle and bridle hanging in a tree and George loose in a pasture. O'Brien was on the lam for eighteen days and then gave himself up. En route back to Deer Lodge, the prison escort treated O'Brien to breakfast and a cigar. Once back in prison, Warden Conley shook O'Brien's hand and commended him for surrendering. Perhaps O'Brien really was innocent. Less than a year later, the governor pardoned him.

Solitary Confinement

CONVICTED of car theft in 1962, Larry Cheadle was a difficult inmate at the Montana State Prison: unruly, disruptive, and known to have mental problems. Cheadle taunted the guards, asking them to put him in "the hole," the dreaded place of solitary confinement. These dungeon-like cells, hollowed out of the bedrock, were terrible places to put a human being. Prisoners entered the cell with a mattress, a pitcher of water, and a bucket for waste. Guards turned the lights off, leaving the windowless spaces pitch dark. Officials claimed not to have used the hole since 1958; inmates, however, disputed that. The guards claimed that they complied with Cheadle to avoid further problems as there was no other place to put him. On Halloween morning in 1966, Larry Cheadle entered the hole.

Six hours later, he was dead. Cheadle's death raised questions. The guards knew he had a heart murmur, but did conditions in the cell contribute to, or cause, Cheadle's death? Hot water pipes to the kitchen, just outside the cell, caused the area to be hot and stuffy. The autopsy revealed that overheating could have caused Cheadle's death, but his death certificate lists acute pulmonary edema, acute dilation of the heart, and a possible epileptic seizure as cause of death. Inmates saw it differently, claiming that Cheadle had been beaten and that guards removed and burned his bloody mattress. One guard believed that Cheadle concealed chloral hydrate tablets in a body cavity and died of an overdose. Regardless of the cause, questions remain and Cheadle's death has become an example that is used in training Montana's corrections personnel to this day.

Turkey Pete

PAUL EITNER was perhaps the Montana State Prison's most colorful character. He was a German immigrant who worked as a porter at a Miles City saloon and lived in a local boardinghouse. One evening in January 1918, Eitner picked up his .38 revolver, strode down the hall, and fired three times at a fellow lodger. The man died three days later. Eitner's motive was never clear. At the last moment in court, he changed his plea from self-defense to guilty, hoping for leniency. The judge gave him life. Eitner was assigned to the state sanitarium at Galen to look after the prison's flock of turkeys. He was thus employed until 1932 when he sold all the birds to a passing farmer for twenty-five cents each. This incident earned him the nickname "Turkey Pete." Eitner believed he had diamond mines and an imaginary fortune. Inmates printed "Eitner Enterprises" on checks in the prison shop, and he gave away millions of pretend dollars. He was mascot to the prison band and acted as manager of the boxing team, shadow boxing his way through every match. The prison board denied him parole a number of times, believing Eitner could not adjust to the outside. In his later years, his prominent nose seemed to grow longer. Its extreme length made lighting his cigarettes potentially dangerous. Paul "Turkey Pete" Eitner died in 1967 at the age of eighty-nine after serving forty-nine years in the state prison. Many mourned his passing and attended his funeral in the prison theater, the only funeral held within the prison walls. His empty cell, #1 in the 1912 cell house, was never reassigned.

On the Home Front and Abroad

Buffalo Soldiers in the Spanish-American War

BLACK regiments stationed and trained in Montana saw service in the Spanish-American War. On January 1, 1898, the entire Tenth Cavalry regiment except for three troops stationed at Fort Keogh* near Miles City assembled at Fort Assinniboine to prepare for combat duty. Three months later, they left for service in the Spanish-American War. The Twenty-fifth Infantry—stationed at Fort Missoula*—had already been deployed for service in Cuba. Blacks made up 25 percent of the American soldiers serving there, and many of them had been stationed at Montana forts. At El Caney, San Juan Hill, and Las Guasimas during this conflict, the buffalo soldiers stepped up and fought at the forefront of the battles. At El Caney, white soldiers refused to fight. Montana-trained black soldiers of the Twenty-fourth Infantry took charge of the front line. At Las Guasimas, black soldiers of the Tenth Cavalry from Forts Assinniboine and Custer fought beside Teddy Roosevelt's famed Rough Riders. Horace Bivins, then a sergeant, operated one of the heavy Hotchkiss guns alone. With each shot, the gun rebounded six to eight feet, and Bivins had to reposition and reload each time. After firing a number of times, the gun was no longer serviceable, and Bivins took up a carbine and went among the Rough Riders, fighting along with them until the battle was over. Today, historians credit these buffalo soldiers with saving the Rough Riders, who got all the press and praise, and Roosevelt, who got himself elected president. An eyewitness to the battle said, "If it had not been for the Negro cavalry, the Rough Riders would have been exterminated."

Civil War Vets

MONTANA'S earliest African American population carried the very real memories of slavery and its associated implications. Most of the first black Montanans were born into slavery or had parents or ancestors who were slaves. Many of them saw service during the Civil War. Upon President Abraham Lincoln's Emancipation Proclamation in 1863, the Union stepped up its recruitment of black volunteers. By the end of the Civil War, roughly 179,000 black men, or 10 percent of the Union Army, had served as soldiers, and another 19,000 had served in the Navy. Nearly 40,000 black soldiers died over the course of the war—30,000 of them succumbed to infection or disease. Black volunteers did many necessary jobs and earned a salary of ten dollars a month, with three dollars deducted for clothing. White soldiers received thirteen dollars a month with no deductions. Three black Union veterans who later made their homes in Montana were Jack Taylor of Virginia City, Moses Hunter of Miles City, and James Wesley Crump of Helena. In the Union Army, Jack Taylor took care of officers' horses and learned the craft of teamster. Moses Hunter reenlisted after the war, served in the Southwest, and by 1939 was eastern Montana's only living Civil War veteran. James Crump lied about his age and joined the Union Army. When his superiors discovered he was only fourteen, he convinced them to let him serve out his three-year term as a drummer. Crump thus was the youngest Civil War veteran in Montana, and because of this, he often carried the flag in parades and he proudly held the flag at the laying of the cornerstone of the Montana State Capitol.

Naval Ships

At least nine naval ships have been christened with names related to the Treasure State. There were three named *Montana*, one named *Montanan*, two named *Missoula*, and four named *Helena*. The first USS *Montana*, launched in 1906, provided escort service during World War I. In 1920 it was rechristened USS *Missoula* after Missoula County. A second USS *Missoula* provided transport service during World War I. Two other ships in the planning stages bore the name *Montana*, but neither of them was built. The USS *Montanan*, a cargo ship launched in 1913, was sunk by a torpedo during World War I. Three of the four USS *Helenas*, named for Montana's capital city, saw wartime action. The first USS *Helena* was a light gunboat launched in 1896. It saw long service during the Philippine Insurrection and World War I and was decommissioned in 1932. The second USS *Helena*, launched in 1938, took a torpedo at Pearl Harbor in 1941 and returned to service to participate in thirteen major naval engagements. It was sunk at the Battle of Kula Gulf in 1943 by Japanese torpedoes, taking 168 of its 900 crew members. It was the first naval ship awarded the Navy Unit Commendation for heroic action. The third USS *Helena* took hits during the Korean War, and as the Seventh Fleet's flagship, it hosted President Dwight D. Eisenhower in 1952. This ship served until its decommission in 1972. Its propeller, anchor, chain, and bell are displayed in Helena's Anchor Park at the south end of Last Chance Gulch. The fourth USS *Helena*, still in service, is a nuclear-powered submarine.

Fort Missoula Internees

After the bombing of Pearl Harbor in 1941, the U.S. government detained thousands of Japanese American and German American citizens, as well as Italian nationals. During this dark period, Fort Missoula was one of the nation's largest internment

Montana Historical Society Photograph Archives, Helena, PAc 2008-112.91

Italian seamen on work release from Fort Missoula where they were interned during World War II.

camps, housing more than one thousand Japanese Americans and as many Italian nationals during World War II. Government officials took Japanese American citizens from their communities, often separated them from family, and sent them to camps like Fort Missoula, far from home. Boards from the detainees' home states considered evidence against them. Future U.S. senator Mike Mansfield served on Montana's board. In the fort's headquarters building, administrative staff processed internees' records and questioned them. A judge presided over so-called loyalty hearings to determine whether the detainees posed a threat to national security. At an average age of sixty, most Japanese detainees were professionals and businessmen from the West Coast. Although the judge found that almost none posed any threat, most remained in U.S. custody for the duration of the war. Detainees were not necessarily mistreated, according to the son of one Fort Missoula internee, but the pain and shame of this experience can never be erased. Recently, a poignant reminder of this tragic episode surfaced. Removal of old carpet in the fort's headquarters building revealed the outline of the judge's bench. From this bench, the judge conducted hearings that decided the fates of Japanese American internees. The courtroom, where so many lives were destroyed, had a disturbing energy that made visitors uncomfortable. At the invitation of fort officials, Zen master Genki Takabayashi of Victor performed a cleansing to release unsettled sprits. However, some believe the ghosts remain.

Ground Observer Corps

THE Ground Observer Corps, or GOC, was a national watchdog organization that grew from the Cold War of the 1950s. The air force created this program as a safeguard against the Soviet attack that never came. This was before radar tracking systems, and the government charged GOC volunteers with reporting low-flying aircraft. Northern border states like Montana were critical. Historian Jon Axline writes that the U.S. military theorized that a Soviet attack would come over the North Pole. Montana was at risk. "Keep watching the skies," said the government. "The Kremlin has 1,000 planes within striking distance of your home." Volunteers proved easy to recruit, and criterion to become a volunteer observer was simple. You had to have normal eyesight and hearing and the ability to speak clearly. Eventually, Montana alone had more than eleven thousand volunteers. Observer stations had to be near a telephone, and volunteers were to watch the skies and listen in two- to four-hour shifts. There was minimal training. A booklet aided in plane identification and a card, held in the air as the aircraft flew overhead, gave an estimated altitude. After brief training, the air force issued each volunteer an impressive Ground Observer Corps patch. Upon sighting or hearing an aircraft, the observer would call the operator and say "aircraft flash." The operator transferred the call to the filter center at Helena or Billings, the observer relayed the information collected, and the filter station then informed the air force. The GOC ended in 1959 when better technology made observers unnecessary. But as Axline sums up, during those unsettled times, the GOC brought communities together and gave citizens a real sense of helping protect the home front.

Japanese Balloons

HISTORIAN Jon Axline tells a story about Oscar Hill and his son, who in 1944 were cutting firewood seventeen miles southwest of Kalispell. They found a strange parachute-like object with Japanese writing and a rising sun symbol stenciled on it. Sheriff Duncan McCarthy took the object to a Kalispell garage. Rumors flew and soon five hundred people crowded into the garage to take a look. It turned out to be a Japanese balloon rigged to carry a bomb. It was the beginning of an aerial attack on the United States by Imperial Japan as World War II wound down. In November 1944, the Japanese began launching hydrogen-filled paper balloons, believing the jet stream would carry them to North America. The attached incendiary and anti-personnel bombs would start forest fires and kill civilians. The Japanese also intended the balloon bombs as psychological weapons, designed to cause confusion and spread panic. The Japanese called them *Fu-Go,* "Windship Weapons." They were the first intercontinental weapons, a low-tech predecessor to the ballistic missiles of the late twentieth century. By April 1945, the Japanese launched over 9,000 balloons. Only 277 reached the United States and Canada. Only one caused injuries, killing five Oregon picnickers when they inadvertently detonated one of the bombs. The project was a failure. A voluntary news blackout in the United States kept the Japanese from discovering if the balloons landed. At least 32 balloon bombs reached Montana between 1944 and 1945. A hiker discovered the last one hanging from a tree southwest of Basin in 1947. Axline points out that balloon bombs in Montana proved that the state was not as isolated and free from world events as the public thought.

Twenty-fifth Infantry Bicycle Corps

BLACK buffalo soldiers of the Twenty-fifth Infantry stationed at Fort Missoula made up the U.S. Army's only Bicycle Corps. Dubbed "iron riders," these dedicated soldiers rode their iron cycles a grueling 1,900 miles from Missoula to St. Louis in 1897, testing the feasibility of troops mounted on bicycles. The Spalding military bicycles were specially made, and fully packed, each weighed about fifty-nine pounds. Each rider carried two days' rations, a bedroll, a leather case, a knapsack, a rifle, and fifty rounds of ammunition. Each bicycle had a drinking cup that fit under the seat. The company included several officers, twenty enlisted men, and a newspaper reporter. The corps had previously taken two preliminary test trips to Glacier and Yellowstone in 1896, totaling 800 miles. They left Missoula for St. Louis on June 14, 1897, and pedaled over snow-dusted peaks and across the sweltering Great Plains. When they arrived

F. J. Haynes, photographer; Haynes Fnd. Coll., Montana Historical Society Photograph Archives, Helena, H-3615

"Iron riders" of the Twenty-fifth Infantry bicycle corps at Mammoth Hot Springs, Yellowstone National Park, October 7, 1897

near St. Louis forty-one days later, a thousand civilian bicyclists rode to meet them and escorted them to town in triumphant celebration. In describing the forty-one-day journey, Lieutenant James Moss reported that the bicycle was thoroughly tested under all possible conditions, except that of being under actual fire. The corps went through a veritable campaign, suffering from thirst, hunger, ill effects of alkali water, cold, heat, and loss of sleep. The army, however, officially decided against forming a permanent bicycle corps. On August 19, 1897, the men of the Bicycle Corps returned to Fort Missoula by rail and the bicycles were shipped back to the Spalding Company.

Mingo Sanders

AFRICAN American buffalo soldiers of the Twenty-fifth Infantry arrived at Fort Missoula in May 1888. Some of these men participated in the famous bicycle experiment, riding 1,900 miles from Missoula to St. Louis in the summer of 1897. One of the key riders was Mingo Sanders, a sixteen-year army veteran. Although partially blind from an explosion, Sanders had an excellent service record and the respect of his white commanding officers. In 1898, the Twenty-fifth was ordered to Cuba at the start of the Spanish-American War. Sanders and the Twenty-fifth distinguished themselves fighting alongside Teddy Roosevelt and his Rough Riders at the Battle of San Juan Hill. Today, historians credit the buffalo soldiers with saving Roosevelt and the Rough Riders, who stole all the credit. Sanders went on to serve in the Philippine Insurrection and received the Medal of Honor for his heroic actions. In 1906, Sanders, stationed at Fort Brown, Texas, was a year away from his retirement and well-deserved pension. He and 166 others of the Twenty-fifth Infantry were falsely accused of murdering a white bartender. Fabricated evidence and President Roosevelt's political agenda led to their dishonorable discharge without a trial, known as the Brownsville Affair. Mingo Sanders, blind in one eye and diabetic, gave most of his life to his country but never received his pension. He died in 1929 during the amputation of a gangrenous foot. Decades later in 1972, Congress reopened the case and found all 167 men innocent. They received honorable discharges posthumously and each soldier won twenty-five thousand dollars in restitution, paid posthumously to his heirs.

Octavia Bridgewater

ALTHOUGH the Army Nurse Corps formed in 1901 and African American nurses served throughout all wars, they served as contract nurses and not in the military. At the end of World War I, when the Spanish flu epidemic caused a severe shortage of nurses, the Army Nurse Corps accepted eighteen African American women after Armistice. They cared for German prisoners of war and African American soldiers stateside but did not serve in wartime. In 1941, the Army Nurse Corps began accepting African American nurses. Due to a quota system, only fifty-six were allowed to join. Slowly, African American nurses pierced the barriers within the military system. One of these nurses was Octavia Bridgewater of Helena. Her father Samuel was wounded in the Spanish-American War, later stationed at Fort Harrison, where he was a cook, and died of his war injuries in 1910. Octavia graduated from the Lincoln School of Nursing in New York in 1930, one of only two nursing schools exclusively for African Americans. She joined the army in 1942. There were at the time eight thousand black nurses in the United States. These women realized that if the military situation was not rectified, black nurses could never be integrated into the mainstream medical community after the war. Nationally through the black press, the women mobilized for their cause. The army and navy lifted the boycott against black nurses in 1945. Octavia earned the rank of captain and returned to civilian life to give many years of service to the Helena community as a pediatric nurse. She was always proud of her role in the national movement that helped pave the way for others.

Ultimate Service

BECAUSE of racial bias and segregation, African American soldiers during World War I did not serve in overseas combat until late in 1917. At that time, backlash from the African American population led the War Department to create the Ninety-second and Ninety-third combat divisions of the 356th Regiment. White officers commanded these black troops, and most of the officers neither prepared the men nor encouraged them to succeed. As was the case in the Spanish-American War, the allies treated American blacks much better than the men's own officers. Gas warfare and poor morale among the troops made this a very nasty conflict. Roy Winburn of Great Falls was one soldier who may have been caught up in racially motivated difficulties. He grew up at Fort Assinniboine, where his father, a buffalo soldier, was garrisoned with the Tenth Cavalry. Roy moved to Great Falls and answered the call for military service in 1917. He served overseas with the American Expeditionary Force and with the 365th Infantry Regiment, Ninety-second Division. The regiment's primary combat occurred at Meuse River–Argonne Forest, a decisive battle in World War I. Although the Ninety-second was criticized for its lack of team spirit and its poor performance, the fault lay with the white officers. The French, however, did not see it that way and decorated these American soldiers for their valor in combat. During combat operations, Private Winburn received wounds from a gas attack and suffered the effects for the rest of his life. He died in August 1951 at age fifty-seven of battle-related illness. He is buried with honors at Highland Cemetery in Great Falls.

UFOs

HISTORIAN Jon Axline has extensively studied and written about a famous incident in 1950. On the morning of August 15, Nick Mariana, the manager of the Great Falls Electrics baseball team, spotted two shiny objects hovering over the Anaconda Company's Black Eagle smelter across the Missouri River from the Legion Ballpark. Mariana captured the two objects on his handheld 16mm movie camera before they sped off and disappeared into the clear blue sky. The grainy film footage is reportedly the first ever shot of unidentified flying objects and is still a mystery. For several weeks, Mariana showed the film to local civic and sports organizations before he submitted it to the U.S. Air Force for further study. At first, the air force offered contradictory explanations when it returned the film to him, but eventually concluded that the objects on the film were probably two fighter jets known to be in the vicinity at the time. Mariana didn't agree with the air force's conclusion and enthusiastically promoted his amazing film for the rest of his life. Private and government investigators periodically interviewed Mariana about the film and what he saw that day in August 1950. Even today, researchers have not determined what the film actually shows. The objects were not reflections of birds, weather balloons, or meteors. They might have been military jets, but most believe they moved too fast and seemed to generate their own light. The grainy film footage is legendary in UFO lore and has never been scientifically explained. Axline concludes that the film may actually be what Mariana claimed it to be—the images of two visitors from outer space.

Medical Missteps and Milestones

Montana's First Doctor

FATHER Anthony Ravalli was a remarkable man of many talents. Born to a wealthy family in Ferrara, Italy, in 1812, he joined the Society of Jesus at fifteen. After Ravalli graduated from medical school, Father Pierre Jean DeSmet recruited him to serve in the Rocky Mountain missions. Father Ravalli arrived at Vancouver, Washington, in 1844, bringing medical supplies, surgical instruments, carpenter's tools, and two heavy millstones. Traveling overland by mule with his precious cargo, he arrived at St. Mary's Mission in the Bitterroot Valley in 1845. With vaccine he brought from Europe, he vaccinated the Salish against smallpox and embarked upon a long life of service. Father Ravalli traveled a two-hundred-mile radius on horseback in the worst weather, ministering to those in need of medical services or spiritual aid. He amputated frozen limbs, delivered babies, nursed Indians and whites through illnesses, and gave last rites to the dying. In 1879, Father Ravalli suffered a paralytic stroke, but still he visited the sick, lying on a cot in a wagon. When he died in 1884, the Montana legislature named Ravalli County in his honor, and he is represented in the Gallery of Outstanding Montanans at the State Capitol. Father Ravalli designed Idaho's famed Cataldo Mission*, a National Historic Landmark, and

St. Mary's Mission, designed by Father Anthony Ravalli, and Ravalli's cabin, which also served as his infirmary. The group gathered with the priest are Salish visiting the tribe's former home in the Bitterroot Valley, circa 1955.

the lovely St. Mary's Mission chapel in Stevensville. St. Mary's statuary, altar carvings, furnishings, and paintings show his creative genius, while his cabin and pharmacy on the Mission's grounds recall his medical skills.

Smallpox Vaccine

SMALLPOX vaccine was among the remedies Lewis and Clark carried in their medical arsenal. Had it not been defective, perhaps it could have lessened future devastation. In the spring of 1837, as the steamer *St. Peters* made its way up the Missouri River from St. Louis, it carried trade goods and something else: passengers and crew sick with smallpox. The captain refused to quarantine the vessel, fearing delays in delivering goods and government annuities. Each stop infected new groups, and within seven weeks, the entire Missouri River Valley had been exposed. Tribes below Fort Pierre in present-day South Dakota had been vaccinated under the federal Vaccination Law of 1832. Congress passed this law after smallpox spread rapidly among the tribes of the central plains in 1831. The disease hit the Pawnees the hardest, claiming three thousand lives and reducing their numbers by half. Doctors vaccinated hundreds of Native Americans along the Missouri River. But the program ended and no tribes above Fort Pierre were vaccinated. Consequently, the tribes of the Upper Missouri were unexposed and vulnerable when the *St. Peters* brought its deadly cargo. Charles Larpenteur was a clerk and trader for the American Fur Company who witnessed the devastation at Fort Union. "It was awful—the scene at the fort," wrote Larpenteur, "where some went crazy, and others were half eaten up by maggots before they died." In the aftermath of the epidemic before the winter snow blanketed the mountains, some estimate the death toll stood at twenty thousand. Smallpox claimed two-thirds of the Blackfeet and more than half the Assiniboines, reducing these powerful tribes to fragments of what they once were.

Scavengers robbed the open-air graves, taking hundreds of buffalo robes that were later shipped for sale on the European market. Yet there is not a single known case of the transmittal of smallpox from these contaminated robes.

Teenage Troubles

In April 1892, Linnie Connor's father marched her, kicking and screaming, down Eighth Avenue in Helena to the House of the Good Shepherd* on Hoback Street. He handed her over to the sisters. The sisters of the House of the Good Shepherd took in fallen women who wished to reform. Neighbors, thus far tolerant of the sisters' mission, were appalled that Linnie's father would forcibly place an innocent child there. They were also aghast that the sisters would accept a fourteen-year-old. But Linnie was incorrigible, and her parents were at their wits' end. As Linnie remained with the sisters into the night, neighbors hung a makeshift likeness of her father in the Connors' front yard and pinned a note on it that read: "C. Connor—Made His Child Homeless." Someone chalked the vigilante warning 3-7-77 on their sidewalk. The next morning, Linnie's parents removed her from the House of the Good Shepherd and placed her with friends. Her father made plans to send her elsewhere. Linnie's friends engaged attorney Ella Knowles, who represented the girl in court. Many neighbors and others testified on her behalf. The judge ruled that Connor was not to lay a hand on his daughter, send her away, or force her to go anywhere against her will without the consent of the court. Some months later, Linnie suddenly died. An autopsy revealed a brain tumor, likely explaining her incorrigibility. Neighbors did not complain when the House of the Good Shepherd moved to Helena's west end in 1909. The complex on Hoback includes a dormitory, chapel, and convent. The only remnant of the House of the Good Shepherd that operated on the west side until the 1960s is the gymnasium, now St. Andrew School.

Buffalo and Brucellosis

THE terrible slaughter of wild buffalo herds in the nineteenth-century West is a well-known and tragic episode. But veterinary microbiologists don't believe that even the huge numbers of buffalo killed account for the animal's extinction. In the end it was disease that brought the buffalo's last gasp. Prior to the introduction of European beef cattle into North America, scientists don't believe that the two most devastating bovine diseases—anthrax and brucellosis—were present among the vast plains' buffalo herds. It is likely that cattle from Texas, driven across the midwestern plains, brought these diseases across unfenced rangelands. Buffalo either came in contact with infected cattle grazing on the vast grasslands or were exposed by passing over the trails cattle had traveled. Exposure of the buffalo to these diseases, however, was only the first part of the chain. Kenneth and Sally Owens, historians and experts on diseases and the environment, suggest that the U.S. government had no qualms about purchasing sickly beef cattle at bargain prices and then distributing the animals to the reservations. Anthrax and brucellosis can be transmitted to humans through contact with infected meat, causing short-term or chronic infections. Known as undulant fever or Malta fever, it can cause miscarriage and sterility. Since women traditionally did the butchering of animals, infection of the buffalo, and later cattle, may have been a factor in diminishing Native American populations in the last quarter of the nineteenth century.

War against Ticks

THE war against Rocky Mountain spotted fever was a battle waged in Montana. It took the contributions of many before science claimed the victory in the 1920s. In 1906, Dr. Howard Ricketts discovered that ticks transmitted the disease, but a vaccine did not come until 1924. In the interim, research began in earnest in 1910. Scientists put themselves at grave risk working under extremely hazardous conditions in the Bitterroot Valley. They set up a laboratory on a homestead where a man had recently died of spotted fever. The cabin was infested with ticks and bedbugs. State entomologist Dr. Robert Cooley was very concerned about the safety of these researchers. Transmission of the disease was not well understood, and Dr. Cooley worried that the recent victim could have been bitten by the bedbugs, which in turn could bite the researchers. No one knew if a bedbug bite could transmit spotted fever. To find out, Dr. Cooley advertised in the *Bozeman Chronicle:* "Wanted: 50 living bedbugs. Will pay $2.00. No questions asked." Cooley got his bedbugs and let them feed on guinea pigs inoculated with spotted fever virus. Then he let the bedbugs bite healthy guinea pigs. To Cooley's great relief, the animals did not develop spotted fever. Among these first researchers was a college student working for the U.S. Biological Survey. He collected 4,500 live ticks for research from 717 animals during that first summer. After his work in Montana, the Biological Survey sent him to Antarctica, where he inadvertently discovered the potential for frozen food. His name was Clarence Birdseye, and he eventually created the modern frozen food industry. His later career path was a far cry from tick research in Montana.

*Rocky Mountain Laboratory**

ROCKY MOUNTAIN spotted fever, or "black measles," fatal in 80 percent of adult cases, plagued early-day settlers in the Bitterroot Valley. In 1906, Howard Ricketts identified ticks as the carriers. In 1910, four researchers began studying ticks in the Bitterroot Valley in an infested cabin where the resident had died of spotted fever. One of these scientists was Clarence Birdseye, later famous as the inventor of Birds Eye frozen foods. In 1912, during the apple boom in the Bitterroot Valley, Governor Edwin Norris advised the

State Board of Health not to publicize spotted fever research, fearing it would hinder agricultural development and adversely impact real estate values. In 1919, Dr. Arthur McCray, state bacteriologist, was working with the spotted fever virus at the laboratory on the capitol campus in Helena when he became infected and subsequently died. Then in 1921, State Senator and Mrs. Tyler Warden of Lolo both died of spotted fever, bringing Montana national publicity. Finally, the U.S. Public Health Service agreed to fund a vaccine development program. In an abandoned schoolhouse converted into a laboratory, doctors Ralph Parker and Roscoe Spencer developed an effective vaccine, but its manufacture required large-scale tick rearing under makeshift conditions. This resulted in tick-related illnesses among the researchers and two deaths. In 1927, the State Legislature authorized construction of the Rocky Mountain Laboratory. It opened in Hamilton in 1928. After World War II, broad-spectrum antibiotics diminished the need for spotted fever vaccination. Today, the Rocky Mountain Laboratories, under government management, are a biosafety level 4 operation using highly pathogenic organisms.

Unsanitary Public Places

MONTANA'S Seventh Legislative Assembly created the State Board of Health of Montana in 1901. Its purpose was to care for the sanitary interests of the people and investigate the relationship of diseases to public habits and localities. Sanitary conditions were in fact deplorable. Montana travelers could expect to find a pump outside most hotels, lodging houses, restaurants, and other public places from which they could draw water for washing and for drinking. Passersby also used these public water sources. You could find a cup to share with fellow travelers and a common roller-type towel that was full of germs. People generally did not consider sanitation, and public habits were terrible. One doctor noted in 1906 that the floors of the day-coach passenger trains were covered with all kinds of filth. "The tobacco chewer," he wrote, "spits on the floor, the little boy throws his peanut hulls on the floor, and the consumptive expectorates on the floor." This was the norm. All manner of refuse accumulated in the coach until the train reached a division point. Then a brakeman would emerge and sweep the floor of the car in a frenzy to keep his schedule, unmindful of the terrible dust and deadly germs he spread. Passengers had to breathe this horrible air; a handkerchief over the mouth was hardly protection. Oftentimes, travelers could not get off the train and had no option but to be bathed in the stifling, choking dirt that swirled in clouds around them. Tuberculosis, smallpox, typhoid, and other diseases were thus spread on public transportation. By 1913, the Board of Health had begun to closely monitor public places and implement rules that finally made people safer.

Student Nurse

AMONG the hundreds of nurses trained by the Montana Deaconess Hospital in Great Falls was Virginia Geiger Kenyon, whose oral interview is in the Montana Historical Society's archives. Virginia studied at the Great Falls Deaconess Hospital from 1932 to 1935. She was seventeen when she began her studies, and the elderly deaconesses—who ran the school and were very strict—terrified her. Students worked twelve-hour shifts and received no compensation until their senior year. Virginia's mother sent her the weekly "cream check," which amounted to about $1.12, and patched her uniforms from discarded pieces and parts found in the hospital laundry room. Students had to attend twelve deliveries of babies before they could graduate, but even then the graduates could not deliver babies on their own. Later in her training, Virginia took a job as public health nurse in Dawson and Wibaux counties. One of her first assignments was to go out into the county and deliver a layette to an expectant mother. As she reached the family's gate, she could hear that the woman was in labor. There were six small children in the house and no other adults. Her husband had gone for the midwife. It was a breech delivery and the baby took a long time getting there. But both mother and child were fine. When Virginia got back to town and reported to the health officer what had happened, he simply mumbled. "Well, the baby would have gotten there anyhow without you." Virginia, on the other hand, felt it was quite an experience! At the time, she was only twenty years old.

Holidays Remembered

Independence Day in Alder Gulch

MUCH has been made of the lines of allegiance drawn in Montana over the Civil War. Little Mollie Sheehan danced for joy with her southern friends upon Lincoln's assassination, and Harriet Sanders wrote of celebrations southern women planned over Lincoln's death. But Julia Gormley tells a little bit different tale about Civil War loyalties in Alder Gulch. When word reached the gold camps about ten days after Lincoln's assassination, stores closed and flags flew at half-mast. There were appropriate speeches and a midnight procession with the band playing a march for the dead. Then, on the Fourth of July that year, with the Civil War over, Julia later recalled that Judge Lott asked her to sing at the Independence Day festivities. She declined but suggested he ask the Forbes sisters, who were good singers. When Judge Lott asked them, they were indignant to have been asked to sing at such a celebration. They were southerners from Missouri who lost their home and suffered greatly at the hands of Union soldiers. Judge Lott returned to Julia and asked her why she had sent him into the rebel camp unprotected. Julia replied that he should not complain since he was not taken captive. Julia confesses that they had a good laugh over the situation. And later, the Forbes sisters did too. Julia goes on to say that she took her children to see the Independence Day parade in

144

Virginia City. "It was really a very fine thing," she wrote, "to see the good feeling between the Southern and Northern people way out there and strangers to each other join so heartily together on that 4th of '65."

Thanksgiving in December

THE first official observance of Thanksgiving after the creation of Montana Territory came in 1865. Although President Lincoln had established the last Thursday of November as Thanksgiving Day, following Lincoln's assassination, President Johnson chose December 7 as the day of official observance. Residents of the mining camps paused in their relentless search for golden treasure and gave thanks for their good luck and for the end of the Civil War. In Virginia City, businesses closed. There were private celebrations and culinary preparations in many homes and restaurants. The *Montana Post* reported that sleighs were gliding merrily around town all day, men hobnobbed at the bars, and there was a singing party in the governor's office. But in many a lonely cabin and isolated homestead, Thanksgiving was a time for memories of other days, loved ones far away, and serious reflection. The next year, 1866, at Last Chance, celebrations were more community oriented. Young ladies put on their pretties and attended the Firemen's Ball on Thanksgiving Eve at the Young America Hall. Markets were well supplied for Thanksgiving Day feasts. Shoppers could choose elk, deer, bear, sage hens, grouse, and pheasant. There was no mention of turkeys, however, at Thanksgiving tables on that particular holiday. In Virginia City, the day was unremarkable. There were no church services, no suspension of labor, and no formal public thanks. The *Montana Post* noted, "When the population of Montana becomes stable, another order will prevail, and Thanksgiving will be greeted with more ceremony." But in private, families gathered at their tables as earnestly and faithfully as if they lived in the States.

Frontier Holiday Fare

OUR holiday menus often include recipes with oysters. That brings to mind the menus our forefathers enjoyed in Montana's most remote mining camps. Oyster suppers were wildly popular in these early settlements. Browsing through the earliest newspapers, you can find mention of oyster suppers served after dances, for church fundraisers, after sleighing parties and other community events, or at other times when a light meal was appropriate. It wasn't until the arrival of the railroad in the mid-1880s that a delicacy like oysters could be delivered fresh. But oysters came in the canned variety and were widely distributed in communities across the western frontier. They could be used in a variety of ways, including oyster stew. The tin can, invented by a Frenchman and patented in 1810, revolutionized food preservation. By the 1830s, lobster canning was a big industry, but it was the Civil War that brought about a need to mass-produce highly portable food with a long shelf life. The first cans were so thick they had to be opened with a hammer. But a thinner can made mass production of canned goods useful for the military. A can opened with a key, like today's sardine cans, was in use by 1866. Canned fruits and meats, including oysters, were readily available by the time the Montana gold rushes were in progress. Field's Steamed Oysters were the most expensive and highly prized of canned goods. In 1864, they sold in Virginia City for $2.00 in gold dust per can, a tidy sum. But by Christmas celebrations in 1867, the price had fallen to about $1.30 a can.

Mining Camp Thanksgiving

ABRAHAM LINCOLN set a precedent during his presidency, proclaiming the national observance of Thanksgiving on the last Thursday in November. In 1863, Harriet and Wilbur

Sanders spent their first Thanksgiving in Montana at Bannack and enjoyed the most remarkable dinner they would ever have. Wilbur Sanders was soon to become famous as a courageous prosecutor, gifted orator, and prominent organizer of Montana's Vigilance Committee. He and his family had come west with his uncle, Henry Edgerton, newly appointed chief justice of Idaho Territory, which then included present-day Montana. En route to the new territorial capital at Lewiston, Idaho, the Edgerton party got as far as Bannack before bad weather ended travel across the Continental Divide. Goods were scarce, freight was slow arriving, and no one even thought about serving a turkey. Next-door neighbors invited Harriet and Wilbur, along with Henry and Mary Edgerton, to Thanksgiving dinner. This neighbor wanted to make a good impression on the politically prominent Edgertons and offered his invitation well ahead of time. He miraculously procured a turkey—an unheard-of and unbelievable luxury—that cost him forty dollars in gold dust. Then he paid a small fortune to have it freighted five hundred miles from Salt Lake City. Harriet wrote later that their Thanksgiving meal in that humble rustic cabin at Bannack was as fine and beautifully prepared as any meal she ever enjoyed in New York City's finest restaurant. Unfortunately, their host failed to make a good impression. In early January, just weeks later, Sanders and the vigilantes saw to the hanging of Sheriff Henry Plummer, the same man who had hosted their Thanksgiving Day feast.

First Montana Christmas

GRANVILLE STUART and his brother James came from California to the Deer Lodge Valley in 1857, before the Montana gold rushes brought the first waves of miners. The Stuarts and their companions, Reece Anderson and Jacob Weeks, claim the honor of making Montana's first recorded gold discovery in 1858. Many years later, Granville recalled their first Christmas in Montana. The four men were living in a skin lodge, camped on the Big Hole River, near the future site of the town of Melrose. That Christmas hardly felt like winter. There was no snow, and the weather was so warm, Granville recalled, that he took his gun on Christmas morning and went out minus his coat after a mountain sheep. Without much effort, he shot a young sheep and carried it back to camp. In the afternoon, Granville followed the Big Hole River a short distance up from camp, where he and his companions had discovered a small hot spring. He banked up a pool of water and took a hot bath under the blue sky. Suddenly, a sharp wind came up from the northwest, carrying a cold winter's bite. He dressed quickly and arrived back at camp nearly frozen, but cleaner than he had been in quite some time. The men enjoyed a hearty Christmas dinner of roast mountain mutton, black coffee, and sourdough bread. There were no vegetables that day, nor were there any all that winter. Soon after Christmas, the coffee ran out and so did the bread, and for the rest of the winter, the men had only an abundance of meat.

Miles City Christmas 1884

MILES CITY looked forward to the holidays in 1884. On Christmas Eve, the *Daily Yellowstone Journal* instructed its readers to "Get the hinges of your jaws ready to warble 'Merry Christmas' to friends and neighbors. And be sure," said the *Journal*, "to clear your chimneys for the descent of Kris Kringle." But not entirely in the Christmas spirit, the *Journal* recorded the final percentile grades of public school students, certainly embarrassing several, including George Busch of the senior class, who earned a 40; Kate Cupples, who earned a 56; and others. Now that's a gift for a parent—to have your child's ill achievement published in the newspaper, and on Christmas Eve. On a more festive note, the *Journal* advertised the perfect Christmas present: the Missouri Steam Washer. No home, said the *Journal*, is complete without it. Patented in 1883, the contraption was so simple to use, claimed the advertisement, that a ten-year-old could do the family wash in an hour. Wouldn't the kids love that present! Or, you could buy a buffalo coat for $15.00, or pantaloons for $1.50. And the *Journal* had some advice on sizing up the roasted Christmas turkey: "Don't look in its mouth as if it were an old horse with a tooth ache," said the *Journal*. "Just gently dislocate its wings. If it's old and tough, you'll have to tug pretty hard on the flappers." When it comes to dessert, said the *Journal,* there will be no poison in your pastry if you use Dr. Price's pure extract of vanilla. So shake the snow out of the Christmas tree and unhinge your jaws for Christmas dinner.

Shopping 1896

SHOPPING is an important part of the holiday season, and that was just as true in 1896. For the holiday meal, shoppers could buy two dozen oranges for thirty-five cents and a gallon of fancy cranberries for thirty-five cents. California wines were twenty-five to forty cents a bottle and "very fine" brandy went for a whopping eighty-five cents. Meat department specials included fresh flounder at ten cents a pound, jackrabbits for twenty-four cents each, quart cans of New York select oysters at thirty-five cents, and freshly skinned perch at three pounds for twenty-five cents. Whole opossums were ninety-five cents each. If holiday shopping brought on a headache, the local drug store could provide a ten-cent bottle of Bromo-Seltzer, and to promote "digestion, cheerfulness, and rest" in children, mothers could count on Castoria; thirty-five doses sold for thirty-five cents. The nasty-tasting brown liquid was a longtime staple. Generations of taste buds—including my own—recoil at the memory of that abominable root-beerish flavored stuff. Advertisements for gifts in 1896 included a muff footstool for the elderly grandmother or aunt. It consisted of a round leather portable footstool, three inches off the ground. A Japanese stove concealed within allowed elderly toes to stay toasty. Another popular item at Christmastime in the 1890s provided a much safer alternative to a Japanese stove. This was the Hot Water Bag, advertised with this poem:

> In winter when it's snowing and the storms are wildly blowing,
> And all the earth is covered o'er with robes of ice and sleet,
> Oh, then our hearts are mellow with compassion for the fellow,
> Who is tortured through the night with his wife's cold feet.

Christmas at the Rio

In December 1935, Helena was still suffering from the Great Depression and the devastation of the recent October earthquakes. The series of temblors left many families in dire need, camping out in their yards for weeks as winter cold set in. Thanksgiving passed with more earthquakes and more terror for the community. Children especially felt the uncertainty of these very bad times. But with the start of the holiday season, people got into the spirit, stores realized good profits, and things began to look better. Movies helped people cope. The Rio Theatre on North Last Chance Gulch had opened the year before, in 1934, and was celebrating its first anniversary. Manager Paul McAddams had an idea for a way to celebrate this special occasion. He teamed up with the Helena Kiwanis to throw a special Christmas party for all the children of Helena. There was a flurry of planning, and Christmas morning dawned cold and clear, and mercifully, the Helena valley was peaceful. As the sun came up, there was a steady procession of children streaming into the theater. After a morning of free comedies, novelties, and cartoons, Santa Claus arrived on the stage, and the Kiwanis Club helped distribute free candy from his pack. McAddams said at the time, "We consider children our best friends as they consistently advertise the shows. Their knowledge of pictures and stars is remarkable. . . . It is our Christmas present to the children of

Rio Theatre, Helena

Helena in celebration of our first anniversary, and we wish them a Merry Christmas." Following the party, movies resumed with continuous showings of *In Person* starring Ginger Rogers.

New Year's Folklore and Traditions

ON New Year's Eve in 1921, the *Columbus News* published a list of superstitions and customs pertaining to this holiday.

Montana is such a melting pot that customs, superstitions, and traditions came from all over the world. Here is a synopsis of some of those: Quiet clear weather on New Year's Eve means the year will be prosperous. But if the wind blows, it is a sign of pestilence. It is lucky to rise early on New Year's Day, but if you wash clothes on the first day of the New Year, you will wash away a friend. If the ice melts on January 1, it will freeze on April 1. While the clock is striking midnight on New Year's Eve, say this poem three times: "St. Anne, St. Anne, send me a man as fast as you can" and you will be engaged within the year. Calling on friends is a longtime tradition on New Year's Day. But in even earlier times, caroling was the custom. Bring the first carol singer who comes to your door on New Year's into your house through the front door, take the caroler throughout the house, and let him out the back door; it will bring luck to your household for the coming year. If the first person you meet on New Year's Day is a man, you'll have good luck. If it's a woman, bad luck. If it's a priest, you'll die within the year; if it's a policeman, you will have a lawsuit. Good luck will come to you if you place coins on your windowsill on New Year's Eve.

New Year's in 1913

ONE of the greatest New Year's celebrations Montana has ever seen took place at Luther Hall in Great Falls in 1913. Nearly one thousand people ushered in the New Year at the Electricians Ball hosted by the electricians' union. The party went on for two nights on New Year's Eve and New Year's night. There was a matinee of silent films sandwiched in between for those who did not care for dancing but wanted to experience the most lavish decorations Great Falls had ever seen. Following a "rose garden" theme, it took forty people to decorate. More than ten thousand roses in white, red, pink, and yellow festooned the hall. Thirteen thousand feet of vines and rose garlands, fastened from above, cascaded to a musicians' pedestal in the center of the hall. Sixty pots of live palms and ferns hung below the balcony, camouflaging the railing in a veritable wall of greenery interspersed with huge pots of American Beauty roses. There were so many roses that the lovely smell perfumed the wintery outdoors all the way down the block. The Great Falls electricians' union accomplished what other groups could not, installing a huge searchlight that played in various colors over the dancing couples while electric signs and several large tungsten lights cast a brilliant glow. The decorating committee spent a whopping $1,200 on their efforts, which was a huge sum for 1913. The *Great Falls Tribune* commented that the decorating committee reached the uttermost heights. It was indeed a fitting celebration for the town famous as the Electric City. On one further note, each lady received a beautiful rosebud at the door, but alas, these were artificial.

Mining Camp New Year's

MARTHA EDGERTON PLASSMAN wrote in 1926 about early New Year's celebrations in Montana and how they evolved as times changed. On New Year's Day at Bannack in 1863, fourteen-year-old Martha and two other young girls set out to keep the custom of visiting. There were few women in the mining camp, and no proper houses to call upon, and so the three stopped at George Chrisman's cabin, then moved down the street to Thompson and Swift's general store. Inside they found Henry Plummer—later hanged by the vigilantes—in an argument with another fellow, both quite inebriated. The conversation was heated, and Mr. Thompson put a hand on Plummer's shoulder, pointing him to the back door. The three teenagers, caught in the middle, made a hasty retreat out the front. Martha was so frightened that she never again stepped inside a store in Bannack. In Virginia City, between Christmas and New Year's of 1867, things were different. The streets were gay with fashionable ladies visiting from house to house. Music and dancing were easy to find, and spirits flowed freely under many hospitable roofs. Nearly ten years later in Helena on New Year's Day 1877, the New York tradition of ladies receiving gentlemen acquaintances was the practice. The newspaper listed the names of ladies receiving callers; several usually went together as hostesses. Dressed in their most beautiful gowns, they received guests throughout the afternoon. Tables were set with the best china and silver and heaped with many kinds of cakes and rolls. But Martha recalled that unlike rough and raw Virginia City, in Helena coffee usually took the place of strong spirits.

Not in Our Town

On December 2, 1993, a brick came hurling through five-year-old Isaac Schnitzer's bedroom window, landing on his bed in a hailstorm of glass. Isaac was fortunately uninjured. Because his bedroom window displayed a menorah, a symbol of the family's celebration of Hanukkah, the Schnitzers had become a target of religious bigotry and vandalism. Montana's early settlement history included a large Jewish population. But lack of economic opportunity prompted most second-generation Jews to move elsewhere. Butte, Great Falls, Billings, and Helena's historic Jewish cemeteries recall these pioneers who helped lay Montana's very cornerstones. But in 1993, the Schnitzers were among the few Jewish families in Billings. Supremacist groups that settled in the Northwest in the 1980s had begun to commit brutal hate crimes against various minorities. Billings suffered desecration of a Jewish cemetery, telephone threats to its Jewish citizens, and swastikas painted on the home of an interracial couple. The Schnitzers were advised to remove the religious symbols from public view. This infringed upon their First Amendment right to religious freedom. News reports left Christians wondering what it would be like if a Christmas tree in the windows of their own homes invited violence.

An idea quickly took root. Menorahs began to appear in thousands of homes in Billings, sending a powerful message of community solidarity. Harassment continued, and some non-Jewish citizens suffered vandalism, but gradually the perpetrators withdrew. The next December, 1994, families in Billings again displayed menorahs, reaffirming their commitment to peace and tolerance. This quiet, courageous message spread and came to be known as the "Not in Our Town" movement. It is a message that continues to reverberate.

Legends and Treasures
of the Treasure State

Medicine Tree

THE Medicine Tree south of Darby on U.S. Highway 93 once towered over the landscape. The three-hundred-year-old ponderosa pine was a timeworn icon, a site sacred to the Salish and Kootenai tribes. According to a legend handed down by local tribes, a monstrous bighorn sheep terrorized the southern Bitterroot Valley. Coyote used his guile to trick the ram into charging a small tree to prove his strength. The ram's large curled horns sank deeply into the trunk and trapped him there. Coyote cut off his head and promised that in the generations to come, there would be no more wicked creatures and the tree would be a place of peace and good luck. But the later stories are just as dramatic. On March 11, 1824, Alexander Ross of the Hudson Bay Company came upon the tree. He wrote in his journal, "Here is a curiosity called the Ram's Horn—out of a large pine five feet from the root projects a ram's head, the horns of which are transfixed to the middle. The natives cannot tell when this took place but tradition says when the first hunter passed this way, he shot an arrow at a mountain ram and wounded him; the animal turned on his assailant who jumped behind a tree. The animal, missing its aim, pierced the tree with his horns and killed himself. The horns are crooked and very large. The tree appears to have grown round the horns." No sign of the ram's head remains today. In 2001, a storm snapped the tree's trunk, leaving only twenty feet of it standing. Vandals poisoned this remaining portion. But travelers still pay homage to the broken trunk, carefully placed a short distance up the hill, with offerings and prayers for good luck.

Big Horn Gun

THE small cannon known as the Big Horn Gun is a Montana treasure with a history that can only be told in part. No one knows exactly what events it witnessed before it came to Montana. Old-timers claimed it saw use in the Mexican-American War in the 1840s, and no one can speculate where it might have been before that. The gun came north on the Santa Fe Trail in 1869 and ended up in Montana Territory, pressed into service accompanying the Big Horn prospecting and exploring expedition from Fort Laramie, Wyoming, to Fort Ellis east of Bozeman. And this is how it became known as the Big Horn Gun. In 1874, the Yellowstone Expedition set off from Bozeman in the dead of winter with 146 men. They carried the cannon on this dangerous trip and used it effectively on several occasions. The next year, when Fort Pease was established as a trading post, the Big Horn Gun was en route to the fort aboard a flatboat. The heavy cannon was not properly secured. It slid forward and back, the boat capsized, and the gun fell into the Yellowstone River and sank to the bottom. It was soon retrieved, oiled, and polished and served until Fort Pease was abandoned in 1876 and the cannon was forgotten. Indians then burned the fort. The gun lay concealed in the ruins, and weeds grew over it. A few years later, Walter Cooper of Bozeman visited the ruins of the fort near the present-day town of Hysham. He stumbled across the cannon and took it back to Bozeman, oiled and polished it, and put it in his armory. A few years later in 1883, the gun rode in the parade welcoming the first Northern Pacific train to Bozeman. In 1935, it sat on the lawn of the new Gallatin County Courthouse*. In 1957, pranksters filled it with rocks and bits of metal and fired it off, breaking windows in the old high school. Today, its belly filled with concrete, the Big Horn Gun has found a final resting place in Bozeman's Pioneer Museum.

Little Rocky Mountains

MANY Indian people believe that spirits dwell in north-central Montana's "island" mountains: the Sweet Grass Hills and the Bears Paw and Little Rocky ranges. Their rugged peaks cluster like tipis in a camp, offering access to the supernatural. The mountains are the nesting place of eagles, the messengers of the spirits who live there. Generations of Blackfeet, Gros Ventres, Assiniboines, and Chippewa-Crees have used these isolated areas for fasting, prayer, and vision-questing. Many Gros Ventre and Assiniboine people still use the Little Rockies for sacred ceremonies. Here the Great Spirit bestowed the precious gifts of water, plants, animals, and solitude. Red willows, sage, and Echinacea found in the prairies in and around the Little Rockies are prized for medicinal and ceremonial purposes. Stories describing the supernatural powers of the Little Rocky Mountains abound. One such story, handed down in many variations, tells of a terrible water serpent that inhabited the spring on Eagle Child Mountain, frightening or even slaying some who attempted to fast there. A White Clay spiritual leader in recent years who went there to fast thought he heard a serpent moving nearby. It frightened him so badly that he abandoned his quest. Another well-known site at the western end of the Little Rockies is a battleground remembered among the northern Montana tribes for its spiritual significance. The great Gros Ventre warrior Red Whip won victory there over the Sioux against incredible odds. His success is attributed to a powerful war charm of otter skin with a bone flute attached and a vision that foretold the battle. Despite the terrible destruction local mining has done, the area remains sacred to Indian people.

Mission Canyon, Little Rockies, southeast of Hayes on the Fort Belknap Indian Reservation, 1946

Sleeping Child Hot Springs

SOUTH of Grantsdale in the Bitterroot Valley lie a small creek and hot springs that are the subject of several legends. One story says that in 1877 when Chief Joseph and his band of Nez Perces came over Lolo Pass into the Bitterroot Valley, they split into two groups. Fleeing General Howard and his soldiers, the two groups traveled separate routes. One group followed a small creek and discovered the beautiful, secluded hot springs. Anticipating a battle, they left their infants at the springs. When they returned, the children, protected by the springs, were all sleeping peacefully. Thus they named the creek and hot springs Sleeping Child. However, another legend is not so pleasant. Earlier stories name the hot springs and creek Weeping Child. Indians of long ago said that when a traveler passed near the springs, a crying child would draw him there. He would find a child weeping uncontrollably and take it in his arms to comfort it. The child would be very hungry, so he would offer his finger as a pacifier. The child was so hungry it soon sucked all the flesh off his finger, then off his arm, and then all the flesh from his body, leaving only a skeleton. The child would then disappear and lie in wait for another unsuspecting traveler to share the same fate. There was a great pile of the bones of all the victims at Weeping Child Hot Springs. Local settlers renamed the springs and creek Sleeping Child, thinking it a better name for such a pastoral place.

Legend of the Bitterroot

MONTANA'S state flower, the bitterroot, miraculously emerges from the runners of its dry root as melting spring snow rehydrates it. Native Americans highly prized the root, using it in trade and for food. The boiled root, although bitter, is highly nutritious. It was one of 134 plant specimens Meriwether Lewis brought to botanist Frederick Pursh upon returning from his explorations.

After several years deprived of soil and water, the dried specimen produced runners. Pursh named it *Lewisia rediviva,* commemorating Lewis and *rediviva,* Latin for "brought back to life." The legend of this plant that sustained native people is, appropriately, a story of resurrection. According to a Salish myth, an old woman left her family to go into the hills to die so her starving children could have her share of food. She stopped by a creek bank, let down her long white hair, and began to sing her death song. The rising sun heard her and recognized her sacrifice. He sent a beautiful guardian bird to watch over and comfort her. The bird told her that that her bitter tears would give birth to a new plant, whose root, as humble as the old woman, would hold the secret of survival. Tears soaking into the root would cause its renewal. When the plant blooms, its flower is as pink as the guardian bird's rosy wing, and its leaves are silver like the old woman's hair. The nourishing root, although bitter as the old woman's tears, holds the promise of renewal. The symbolism is twofold. The flower is a feast for the eyes while its humble root is a feast for the body.

Stained Glass Artistry

THE fifty-nine stained glass windows in the capital city's St. Helena Cathedral* are a rare and irreplaceable collection of imported German art. The firm of F. X. Zettler, whose exquisite "Munich style" glasswork is found in St. Peter's Basilica at Vatican City in Rome, crafted the windows between 1908 and 1926. These windows tell the stories of historical events and recall the Middle Ages when most people could not read. Pictures of Christian teachings served as the "Bible of the Poor." But the exquisite pictorial style of Zettler's studio blended nineteenth-century Romantic and German Baroque styles with Italian Renaissance artistry. Painting on large sheets of glass and firing them at high heat allowed fantastic portraiture and detail. The leaded seams of the Munich style do not interrupt the scene but are part of it. Zettler's paintings are multidimensional. Even the plants have such miniscule detail that the flowers and foliage can be botanically identified. Zettler windows are still in place in many American cathedrals, but the artist himself believed that St. Helena's windows were the finest his company ever turned out. In 1982, stained glass expert Father Dan Hillen began restoration of St. Helena's windows. The glass had suffered damage, especially in 1935 when earthquakes rattled the area. Father Hillen uncovered and repaired over one hundred broken pieces that had been patched with window glass and touched up with house paint. Careful maintenance remains ongoing. Many artists copied Zettler's work, and without a signature it is difficult to authenticate. The company signature of F. X. Zettler, however, appears in the first panel to the left in the Cathedral's foyer, authenticating St. Helena's irreplaceable treasures.

Butte Hangings

COPPER veins fueled the city of Butte, where copper kings amassed wealth as thousands toiled in the treacherous underground. Mining left a spectral legacy. Among Butte's many haunted places is the Butte–Silver Bow County Courthouse*. After hours, the elevator goes up and down, its buttons pushed by ghostly fingers. It stops, the doors open to discharge its unseen passengers, the doors softly close, and the elevator goes on its way. Workers report footsteps echoing through the lofty halls, books falling off shelves, and a shadowy figure that wanders through the empty spaces. He turns abruptly and walks through the walls. Silver Bow County government has occupied the site since Montana became a state, and it has seen multiple executions. Between 1889 and 1926, ten men faced the hangman in the jail yard. One of these was Miles Fuller, convicted in 1906 of the gruesome murder of Henry Gallahan. Fuller, an elderly and feeble old prospector, never admitted guilt. A bizarre thunder-clap ominously punctuated his swift execution. After the present building replaced the first courthouse in 1910, deputies in the jail's sleeping quarters claimed to see Fuller's ghost. Others reported a shadowy figure in the locked yard. Although Fuller was unknown to them, witnesses described him perfectly, down to his long beard and tattered hat. Legend has it that Fuller, or whoever he is, roams the courthouse corridors in a curious pattern. Based on many eyewit-nesses' accounts, Mark Reavis, a former Silver Bow County historic preservation officer, is convinced that the spectral visitor follows the floor plan of the former building.

Old Man Stormit

THERE is a butte in south-central Montana's Carbon County known as Stormit Butte, named after J. P. Stormit, a color-ful old-time cowboy. He was a rough, unkempt man who sported a four-foot beard stained with tobacco juice. His shack sat above Cherry Springs four miles south of the butte. Locals say that Old Man Stormit had a herd of Thoroughbred stallions acquired from Marcus Daly's famous stock. He brought them to graze below the butte and spent his time camped out on high, watching over them. Hunched down over the edge above the sweeping view, Stormit kept constant watch for rustlers. He loved those horses with a fierceness that matched his gaze. Locals claimed his strange, glittering eyes looked right through you, even in the dark. A startling photograph of J. P. Stormit in a local history, compiled by the Joliet 4-H Club, proves that Old Man Stormit indeed had incredible piercing eyes. He rode the range with his herd, racing after them, his long beard flowing behind him, his eyes glittering, his cackling laughter echo-ing in the wind. On stormy nights he would be out gathering his herd, riding out the weather with them, his yellow-orange lantern light swaying in the wind. When Old Man Stormit died in 1898, there was no ceremony, no eulogy. Neighbors covered him with his bedroll and laid him in the ground atop the butte. His yellow-orange lantern light is sometimes visible moving on the butte. It disappears and reappears in a different spot. When a storm gathers, Old Man Stormit's cackle rises on the wind and his thundering herd of ghost horses rumbles across the valley.

From Steamboats to Skunkwagons

Titanic *Memory*

TWENTY-YEAR-OLD Mary Lawrence left Austrian Hungary, employed as a maid to a physician's family en route to America. Mary seldom spoke about her terrible ordeal aboard the ill-fated *Titanic*, but in 1939, she did describe her experience to a news reporter. She recalled the utter horror of that night, April 15, 1912. First she heard a terrible crunching sound, then people running, screaming, crying, and shoving and pushing. She saw many fall overboard, and she saw her employer—the doctor—and his wife and their three children—all go over the side of the huge ship and into the water. She jumped from the sinking ship into a boat, suffering a severe and permanent injury to her leg as she landed. All around her, people were drowning in the ice-cold water. She recalled crowding into the lifeboat, and several people froze to death during the five hours before help came. She could not remember the rescue, but once she arrived at New York City, Mary recalled wandering the streets aimlessly, dazed, homeless, injured, and unable to speak English. After several weeks, she finally met someone from her native homeland who helped her find work on a farm. Several months later, she learned of an uncle in Montana. Mary traveled to Dillon and stayed with her uncle there for several years. In 1915, she married Jacob Skender, a miner and smelter worker. The Skenders settled in the Butte neighborhood of Meaderville, where they raised six children, but Mary could never put aside that terrible experience. There were more than 2,200 people on the *Titanic's* maiden voyage. Of those, Mary Lawrence Skender was one of 705 survivors.

Stagecoach Tips

THE *Omaha Herald* published a list of tips and etiquette for stagecoach travelers in 1866. These underscore the fact that travel on the Montana frontier, and even in more civilized places, was not like it is today. Stage stops were usually dirty and the food terrible. But the rest stops, nasty as they were, offered welcome respite from the rigors of jostling inside the coach. The first rule, warned the paper, is not to wear tight-fitting boots, shoes, or gloves in cold weather. If the team runs away, don't jump out, because you will get hurt. Don't drink spirits when on the road in cold weather because you will freeze more quickly if you are under the influence. Don't complain about the food at the stage stops; stage companies provide the best they can. Expect the most primitive sleeping arrangements if your journey calls for overnight at a stage stop. Don't keep the stage waiting, and don't smoke a strong pipe inside the coach. Be sure to spit on the leeward side or you—or your companions—will get it back in the face. If you have anything to drink in a bottle, pass it around to all in the coach. Procure your liquor before starting on your trip as ranch whiskey is not nectar of the gods. Don't swear or lop over your neighbors when you sleep. Take small change to pay expenses, and never shoot on the road as the noise might frighten the horses. Don't discuss politics or religion. Don't point out where murders have been committed, especially if there are women passengers. Don't lag at the wash basin. Don't grease your hair, because travel is dusty. Don't imagine for a moment that you are going on a picnic. Expect annoyances, discomfort, and some hardship. And of course, have a safe trip.

Safe Crossing

IRISH-BORN Christopher P. Higgins came to the United States at eighteen and joined the army. In 1853, he helped survey the Northern Pacific Railroad's route under Governor Isaac Stevens of Washington Territory. In 1855, Higgins was with the Stevens expedition that came to Montana to negotiate the Hellgate Treaty at Council Grove. During this expedition, Stevens's party arrived where St. Regis is today. The river was at flood stage, 150 yards wide. The men set to building rafts to get across. As they worked, a band of Indians amazed the men by crossing the river without rafts. They spread their buffalo hide lodge coverings along the river bank, piled blankets, provisions, and equipment on them, drew up the four corners, and tied them securely like laundry in a sheet. They placed all the bundles in the water. Women, children, and dogs calmly climbed on top. The men then swam their horses across, towing the bundles. Stevens's men went on building their rafts. Two of the three made it safely across the river, but the third and largest carried the governor. The current swept the raft downstream. Higgins leapt into the river and grabbed a pack rope attached to the raft. He swam back to the riverbank and flung the rope around a tree to tether it, saving not only the raft but also Governor Stevens. Upon retiring from the army in 1860, Higgins returned to Montana. In partnership with Francis Worden, he established the Hell Gate Trading Post along the Mullan Road; Hell Gate became the first settlement in the Missoula area.

Steamer Chippewa

THE first two steamboats to navigate the Missouri River all the way up to Fort Benton were the *Chippewa* and the *Key West*. These side-wheel steamers made history when they opened a new route to Oregon that was faster than the Oregon Trail. Under contract with Pierre Chouteau of the American Fur Company, the two steamers carried five hundred tons of freight between them. They also transported 350 military men who were to meet Lt. John Mullan at Fort Benton and travel over his new wagon road to Walla Walla, Washington. Along with a third vessel, the *Spread Eagle,* it was the largest fleet to depart for the Upper Missouri. St. Louis gave the steamers a resounding sendoff on May 3, 1860. The voyage was uneventful. At the mouth of the Milk River, roughly where Fort Peck is today, the *Spread Eagle* transferred its freight to the other two, and the heavily laden *Chippewa* and *Key West,* their decks swarming with soldiers, proceeded on to dock at Fort Benton on July 2, a journey of thirty days. The next year, the American Fur Company counted on the *Chippewa* and the *Spread Eagle* to transport goods. The two departed St. Louis for a second trip to Benton. The overloaded *Chippewa* was doomed when a deck hand took a candle into the hold to tap off a keg of alcohol, igniting it. Pandemonium ensued. The passengers scrambled safely onto shore, and the boat was cast adrift. Tons of gunpowder caused a terrific explosion an hour later. Among the lost freight were fifty-seven tons of Blackfeet annuities and seven thousand dollars' worth of merchandise for Frank Worden's mercantile at Hell Gate. Afterward, the site of the accident near present-day Poplar was known as Disaster Bend.

The Josephine *Conquers the* Yellowstone

THE U.S. government tested navigation on the Yellowstone in 1875. Because of its gravel bed, its stable banks and islands, and its freedom from snags, Lieutenant Colonels J. W. Forsyth and F. D. Grant were convinced that the Yellowstone offered a better highway for commerce than the Missouri River. The army chartered the steamer *Josephine* under Captain Grant Marsh to test the theory in the late spring of 1875. The *Josephine* steamed along until she was twenty-five miles above the mouth of the Big Horn River. Rugged bluffs then closed in as the current increased in depth and speed. It became a struggle between boat and current. The *Josephine* needed every pound of steam her boilers could muster, and as her paddle-wheel beat the water into foam, it seemed that she was standing still. After a battle lasting several hours, the *Josephine* emerged from the narrows into a wider channel. Steaming was easier, and soon Pompey's Pillar*, the landmark made famous by Lewis and Clark, came in sight. The crew enthusiastically climbed the monument and found Clark's signature with the date July 25, 1806—its etched letters as clear as if they had just been carved. Soldiers and crew followed suit, inscribing their names, and Captain Marsh added the date, June 3, 1875. Resuming the journey, the steamer struggled against the increasingly swift current and treacherous rapids. After several difficult days, the current became so strong that the *Josephine* had to turn back. The steamer made it as far as the future site of Billings. Navigation was plausible, but the advent of the railroad soon nullified this conquest.

Lincoln County Ferry Goes A.W.O.L.

FERRIES were indispensable to early-day Montanans, especially in sparsely populated and isolated places where it was too expensive to build bridges. The *Troy Herald* of June 3, 1910, reported an accident that left the Troy Ferry across the Kootenai River in Lincoln County missing and out of commission for a good long while. The ferryman anchored the boat on the north shore and left on some errand. A foolhardy pedestrian did not want to wait. He decided to take matters into his own hands and cast the boat adrift. He jumped aboard, apparently expecting the boat to guide itself across the river. Instead, the swift-flowing water hit the boat broadside and tore the cable loose. Away went the boat and its passenger, yelling at the top of his lungs, speeding down the river. Some branches briefly detained the ferry, and the passenger scrambled off onto the riverbank. Then the river again swept the boat away, and off it went speeding down the river as if it were in a race. The passenger no doubt reached safety, but he never showed his face in Troy and his identity remained in question. However, witnesses a short distance downstream saw a man crossing the river in a rowboat. A few hours later, the ferry whizzed by the community of Leonia as if it were trying to break some record; it disappeared on its way to parts unknown. Lincoln County was left without transportation across the river at Troy until a new boat could be built. The *Herald* speculated that the errant ferry was probably still speeding its way through British Columbia.

Train Wreck at Boulder

At four o'clock on the afternoon of October 15, 1890, a train laden with ore on the Northern Pacific's Helena, Boulder Valley & Butte Railroad chugged south along its rugged route from Helena to Boulder. Samuel T. Hauser filed articles of incorporation, with himself as president, and financed the line, built in 1887. Although intended to enter Butte, the line never extended to Butte and ended at Calvin. On that October day in 1896, the locomotive, four freight cars full of ore, and a caboose made their way up the nine miles to the summit of Boulder Hill at the Zenith station. This rugged route consisted of three short tunnels, several wooden trestles on a 3 percent grade, and several sixteen-degree curves. The train was moving at no more than ten miles per hour as regulations required. As the train passed over the first bridge south of the Zenith station, the trestle collapsed beneath it and the train fell into the ravine below. The caboose and one of the ore cars landed upright. Miraculously the only injury was a broken arm, but for engineer H. H. Mayhew and his seven-man crew, the accident was a horrific event. Mayhew was so traumatized he could not work and sued the railroad. He used his five-thousand-dollar settlement to open a cigar store in Anaconda. Northern Pacific investigators determined that the bridge design was not faulty. Rather, after the trestle was constructed, workers forgot to tighten the bolts. Northern Pacific maintenance crews spent the next several weeks tightening bolts on all the other trestles on the Helena, Boulder Valley & Butte line.

James J. Hill's Legacy

GREAT Northern Railway mogul James J. Hill left ten grown children and many grandchildren when he died in 1916. He also left a fortune valued at between $100 and $300 million. The greatest part of his wealth lay in stocks in the Great Northern, Northern Pacific, and Burlington Railways. Upon Hill's death, his descendants assumed his business interests. A decade after his death, two of his grandchildren, Louis Hill Jr. and G. N. Slade, carried on their grandfather's legacy working for the railroad. In 1927, the two young men were passing through Missoula on their way west to the coast. Slade was an assistant division trainmaster, while young Hill had begun working at the bottom of the ladder, starting with a section gang to learn the ropes. He was moving up to a higher-level job and thus was traveling through Montana en route to assume this new position. The *Daily Missoulian* reported that the cousins stood on the Northern Pacific platform waiting to board the North Coast Limited. Time got away from them as they chatted with officials. The train began to pull out. They each dashed for a Pullman car to find the steps pulled up and the doors locked. Slade pounded on his door and the porter let him in. But Hill was not so lucky. He was left hanging onto the door handle as the train gathered speed. He made a very lucky dive for the open door through which his cousin had gone, caught the handle, and disappeared inside flashing a grin. The *Missoulian* pointed out that trains must keep their schedules and won't stop even for those who own them.

Aviation History

🏵 EUGENE ELY and Cromwell Dixon celebrated aviation firsts in Montana in 1911, and ironically, both young pilots met tragic ends soon after. Twenty-five-year-old Ely was already famous as the first pilot to take off and land on a naval ship. The well-known aviator was also the first to fly an airplane in Missoula. On June 28, 1911, he took off and landed at the baseball field at Fort Missoula. He made three successful flights, the third with his mechanic as a passenger. It was the first dual flight in Montana. His Curtiss Pusher airplane arrived at the Missoula depot by train after similar flights in Butte, Great Falls, Kalispell, and Lewistown. To transport excited spectators to the fort for the event, both the railroad from the Bitterroot Valley and the Missoula streetcar line added extra cars. Over three thousand people witnessed the flight. On October 18, 1911, at the Georgia State Fair in Macon, Georgia, Ely died after jumping from his plane as it crashed. In Helena, Cromwell Dixon made headlines that same year. On September 30, spectators watched him take off from the fairgrounds and land on the west side of Mullan Pass, becoming the first aviator to cross the Continental Divide. Days

Cromwell Dixon at the controls of the *Hummingbird*, after crossing the Continental Divide

later, on October 2, Dixon died when his plane crashed at the state fair at Spokane, Washington. Both pilots died within two weeks of each other, having made aviation history in Montana.

Stoner Transportation Company

JULIUS STONER came to Montana in 1896 to work in the mines at Marysville. He later ranched, and in 1927 he got the mail contract for Lincoln and drove the route to Helena and back again. At that time, the motorized vehicle used on the route was called "the stage." The Stoner family also had a store and gas station in Lincoln. Julius drove the mail route over Stemple Pass. He hauled freight as well as passengers and operated Stoner's Halfway House at the top of the pass from the 1920s until the end of the 1930s. When the mountain road became impassable during the winter, Stoner switched to a sleigh and horses. Baggage, passengers, and freight would be transferred from the vehicle to horses at the halfway house. The Stoners were very innovative. Eventually, Julius and his son George made the first ski-equipped stage—the forerunner of the snow cat—to carry the mail over Stemple Pass. After they created their "snow cat," they did not use horses anymore. To craft the vehicle, they used an old Model A Ford. They removed the rear fenders and added an axle and wheels mounted ahead of the rear drive near the vehicle's center. They placed narrow, metal caterpillar treads around the two wheels on each side of the vehicle. Skis were mounted on the front steering gear. When Julius retired, his son George drove the route until 1947.

A. J. Gibson's Fatal Attraction

A. J. GIBSON was the architect of many homes and buildings in southwestern Montana, including the Daly Mansion in Hamilton and the Missoula County Courthouse*. Gibson was born in Ohio and attended school only sporadically. But he was a genius when it came to using tools. At eighteen, he built the family barn, cutting each piece of wood by hand. The pieces fit together perfectly. Gibson came to Butte in 1883 after the death of his father. He moved to Missoula in 1889 and briefly practiced carpentry. Entirely self-taught with a legacy of over ninety buildings, his productivity as an architect in practice for only eighteen years is remarkable. He retired in 1909 at only forty-seven. Gibson was an automobile enthusiast from the very beginning of the auto industry. In 1902, he bought one of the first cars in Missoula and organized the town's first automobile club. He and his wife, Maud, had a great time traveling and camping when cars were novelties and roads little more than trails. They traveled extensively on the West Coast, were the first Montanans to cross both the Canadian and Mexican borders, and drove to New York in perhaps the first cross-country trip by automobile, although part of the trip was actually by rail. Ironically, it was an automobile accident that took his life. Gibson was partially deaf, and on New Year's Eve in 1927, he apparently failed to hear the train's whistle. The car's windows were frosted over, and the Gibsons could not see the approaching train. They were killed instantly as they crossed the tracks on Dakota Street in Missoula in the path of an oncoming locomotive.

Charlie Russell's Hearse

On October 28, 1926, cowboy artist Charles Marion Russell's funeral made headlines across the state. He was buried as he lived, a wrangler at heart and a gentle soul whose many friendships knew no bounds. Fellow wrangler Horace Brewster recalled that in all his life Russell "never swung a mean loop, never done dirt to man or animal." As mourners said good-bye at a Great Falls cemetery, a cloud with a golden rim cast a glow across the landscape, spreading colors that matched those Russell captured in his many canvases. Some months before, Russell had undergone surgery and told his wife that when the end came, he wanted to be transported to the cemetery behind horses. Russell hated automobiles and never learned to drive. He called them "skunkwagons" and wanted none of that for his last ride. He came through the surgery fine but suffered a fatal heart attack some months later. Businesses closed and flags all over Great Falls flew at half-mast in tribute to the artist whose landscapes and scenes preserved the fading cowboy lifestyle. To honor his wishes, his wife, Nancy, located a horse-drawn hearse in Cascade that had been in storage for fifteen years. The hearse carried Russell's remains to Highland Cemetery while his saddled but riderless horse followed. It was a fitting farewell to a beloved Montanan. The hearse went back into storage until 1946 when Charles Bovey, who was collecting artifacts for his tourist operation at Virginia City, purchased it. It again lay in storage at Nevada City until the Bovey estate donated it to the C. M. Russell Museum in Great Falls, where it is on display.

Impressing Visitors Then and Now

Central Park

BUTTE had its Columbia Gardens, but few recall that Helena too had a recreational mecca. Brothers Frank and Joseph Mares opened Central Park west of town in 1895. The electric trolley system carried visitors to the sprawling grounds. The park, along with the Broadwater Hotel, Kessler Brewery, State Nursery, and Fort Harrison, once made up an important historic complex. Central Park had something for everyone. There was a dance pavilion, picnic areas, two restaurants, two saloons, bowling alleys, a fabulous merry-go-round, a zoo, and a league-sized baseball field and grandstand. Tom Mills, whose State Nursery was close by, did the exquisite landscaping. Peacocks and swans roamed freely among the crowds. The zoo included monkeys, bears, coyotes, open rabbit pens, and a domed aviary for eagles, owls, and other native birds. The tracks of the Northern Pacific Railroad ran next to the park. Passenger trains slowed down to show off Montana's game animals, such as elk, deer, and buffalo, pastured in an enclosure along the tracks. Also along the railroad right-of-way, adjacent to the park, a handful of Indian families living in tipis added another element to the scenery. The Mares brothers made their fortune in the meat-packing business and operated a large-scale slaughterhouse on acreage along Ten Mile Creek. Central Park's manmade lake not only served recreational purposes but in the winter also supplied ice necessary for the Mareses' refrigerated warehouse. Joseph Mares's death in 1926, Prohibition, and the discontinuation of trolley service brought closure to Central Park. In 1943, the grounds became the Green Meadow Country Club.

Brush Lake

BRUSH LAKE east of Plentywood is a spring-fed lake created as receding glaciers exposed a deep depression ten thousand years ago. A mile long and sixty-five feet at its deepest, the crystal clear lake is a place of danger and mystery. Hans Christian Hansen filed a homestead claim in 1914 and built the Brush Lake Summer Resort to attract local families. But the following year, a boating accident on the lake took the lives of Hansen and his wife. Under new owners, the resort's peak popularity came during Prohibition, when libations smuggled from Canada flowed freely. The lake's clear water makes it attractive to professional divers who come to hone their skills. One group of experienced divers, who had worked in recovery efforts throughout the world, claimed that, as they explored the lake's bottom, they all heard sand crabs. These are small insects that live in salt water. The only other place these divers had heard the strange chirping of sand crabs was in the Pacific Ocean. It is also odd that Brush Lake's clear water has never sustained a fish population. It has been stocked, but scientists believe that the fish die off because oxygen levels are too low. The lake has seen more than its share of deaths. An accident in 1948 took the lives of seven boaters; altogether, eleven people have lost their lives in Brush Lake. Despite posted warnings, it is still a popular recreation area. Its north end is a state park, while the south end, where partygoers once danced the night away, is now quietly under private ownership.

Beattie Park*

PIE-SHAPED Beattie Park in Helena's Sixth Ward once was a busy business block with a saloon, a hotel, two Chinese laundries, a barber shop, and a meat market. But by 1929, the buildings had become seedy and abandoned, and the area was infamous as the worst-looking spot on the entire Northern Pacific line. The city decided to do something about it. They used a pot of money given by the Beattie family of Illinois in memory of the three Beattie brothers who were early Helena businessmen. Alexander Beattie was one of the first to invest in the small commercial hub that quickly grew to serve the Northern Pacific upon its arrival in 1883. The ground floor of his three-story Grand Pacific Hotel still stands at the east end of the Larson Block* on Railroad Avenue. The 1935 earthquakes claimed its two upper stories. Beattie was a Union officer in the Civil War. He carried a bullet lodged in his body from the Battle of Stones Ridge. In the spring of 1884, as his hotel was doing a lucrative business, Beattie, an attorney and district court clerk, married Maggie Carroll. A few months later, Beattie fell ill and suddenly died from that Civil War bullet. His will named Maggie and his two brothers, Edward and George, joint and equal heirs. The brothers came to Helena to manage his affairs, buying out Maggie's third interest for thirty thousand dollars. However, Maggie discovered several years later that the brothers had duped her and she should have realized three times the amount. These family politics have been forgotten, but Beattie Park remains one of Helena's loveliest urban retreats.

Judith River Ranger Station*

THIRTEEN scenic miles south of Utica, in a clearing adjacent to the swift-flowing Middle Fork of the Judith River, the beautifully restored Judith River Ranger Station is a perfect family getaway. A night or a week in this homey retreat is an unforgettable experience. Forest Service ranger Thomas Guy Myers took up residence in the newly created Highwood Mountains Forest Reserve (now part of the Lewis and Clark National Forest) in 1906. He set to building a field office and home using a catalog-ordered house kit supplemented with native logs. Myers married Emily McLaury in the early 1910s and brought her to the station. The couple raised their son Robert at the station, and Emily taught school. The family lived there year-round until the early 1930s. When Forest Service preservationists began extensive restoration, carpenters made wonderful discoveries. They found a teaching tool forgotten beneath a layer of sheetrock in young Robert's upstairs bedroom. A historic timeline Emily drew on the wallpaper depicts the Stone Age and ancient Mediterranean history. Ranger Myers recycled everything. The house kit's shipping crate framed the living and dining room doorway; wallpaper samples and opened mail filled in gaps around the windows and doors. Today, visitors who step across the threshold trade electricity and running water for a rare opportunity to live as the Myers family did a century ago. Contact the Forest Service office in Stanford about renting this historic home.

LaHood Park

ONCE upon a time, motorists on U.S. Highway 10 east of Cardwell stopped to gas up, grab a bite, or get a room at the LaHood Hotel. Located at the head of the scenic Jefferson River Canyon, the complex offered a fantastic panoramic view. Shadan "Dan" LaHood built his Mountain View Inn in 1929, and by 1933 he added some tourist cabins across the way. He named his little town LaHood Park. A few years later, LaHood commissioned Butte sign painter Frank Bliss to paint panels on the underside of his gas pump island canopy in front of the hotel. The panels provided a detailed map of U.S. 10, scenes from nearby Lewis and Clark Caverns, and various advertisements for other local attractions like Gregson and Boulder hot springs and various businesses. There were also colorful advertisements for Butte and Highlander beers. One panel proclaimed LaHood's political leanings. It read: "President F. D. Roosevelt for the New Deal, Shadan LaHood for the New Idea and Montana Booster." In 1950, LaHood constructed a separate restaurant adjacent to the hotel and converted the tourist cabins into the Lewis and Clark Lodge Motel. LaHood Park continued to do a thriving business on the highway well into the 1950s. Dan LaHood died in Butte in 1957, and other owners tried to keep LaHood Park going. But in 1966, the construction of Interstate 90 approximately three miles north bypassed LaHood's complex. The paintings under the canopy remained intact and were a curiosity for those who pulled over to view them. In 2001, fire destroyed the hotel and the signs, taking with it Dan LaHood's unique legacy.

Laurel Roadside Museum

DESPITE the Great Depression, thousands of Americans took to the roads in the 1930s. To lure tourists to Montana, the Montana Highway Department's Robert Fletcher developed an ambitious promotional program. It included publishing the first highway map in 1934; creating a historical highway marker program in 1935; constructing roadside picnic areas, information centers, and port-of-entry stations; acquiring Pictograph Cave outside of Billings; and establishing a roadside museum program. Fletcher envisioned a chain of roadside museums constructed by the highway department but staffed and maintained by local chambers of commerce. Laurel was the only community that took advantage of this idea. The museum building, also housing the city police department, opened in 1938. Fletcher built the exhibit cases to display artifacts from Pictograph Cave. The department's graphic artist, Irvin "Shorty" Shope, created wonderful dioramas. Other exhibits included fossils, dinosaur bones, and a large mounted bison head loaned by local businessmen. The Laurel Commercial Club hired Max Big Man, a Crow Indian from the Hardin area, to curate the museum and provide lectures on Indian life to tourists. He and his family lived in two tipis nearby. A black bear named Susie lived in a cage between them. The seasonal museum was a popular attraction until World War II led to loss of funding and its closure in 1941. What happened to the museum's exhibits and displays is a mystery. The building, however, is an important element in the Laurel Historic District* and is still in use as the Laurel Chamber of Commerce*.

Eagle's Store*

WHEN the tracks of the Oregon Short Line reached West Yellowstone in November 1907, park employee Samuel P. Eagle applied for and was granted a permit to operate a business adjacent to the railway right-of-way. The Eagles, in partnership with the Alex Stuarts, built a tiny twelve- by twelve-foot general store on the site in 1908. It was the first commercial operation in West Yellowstone. The Eagles enlarged the store in 1913, and in 1927 the old store was razed and construction began on the present building. It was built in three stages and finished in 1930. Prominent Bozeman architect Fred Willson, who designed other structures in the same rustic style within Yellowstone National Park, designed all three sections. Donating his time because of a desire to promote the rustic style, Willson was reimbursed for direct costs only. Massive eighteen- to thirty-six-foot red fir logs set in rhyolite and concrete support the building. Shingle siding and a roof of multicolored T-lock asphalt shingles pierced by gabled dormers provide striking surface variation. All elements of the three sections are original. Outstanding interior features include the back bar installed in the original store in 1910 and the original 1930 front bar and stools. Millwork, tile, and white marble tops of both the customer counter and the back bar remain intact. Still a gift shop and soda fountain owned and managed by the Eagles, this impressive pioneer family business is one of West Yellowstone's most outstanding architectural landmarks and a must-see for visitors.

Lewis and Clark Caverns

On a winter day in 1892, hunters Tom Williams and Bert Pannell noticed a curious curl of smoke coming from a mountainside. The two climbed with difficulty and when they reached the source, they found that it was actually steam coming from a hole in the ground. They cast rocks into the hole and marveled at the echoes, realizing they had discovered a huge cave. The steam was pushed out from deep within, and just like in living things, you could see its breath on this cold winter day. Six years later, Williams and Pannell returned with candles, ropes, and friends to explore their tantalizing discovery. The cave, full of passageways, rooms, and torturous openings, was six hundred feet long and four hundred feet deep. Stalactites and stalagmites in a marvelous profusion of terraces and cascades decorated its floors, ceilings, and walls. Various drip formations enhanced the wild, natural beauty. Miner Dan Morrison figured people would pay to see the cave and staked a claim there. He added a trail, built two thousand wooden steps to the cave, widened the entrance, and took paying tourists on tours. But the Northern Pacific Railroad took him to court, claiming ownership, and won. Then it turned the cave over to the federal government. In 1908, President Theodore Roosevelt named the cave for explorers Lewis and Clark because part of their route was visible from the cave's entrance. Morrison led tourists to the cave until the day he died in 1932, defying government ownership. After Morrison's death, the federal government added electricity and other improvements and gave ownership to the State of Montana. Lewis and Clark Caverns became Montana's first state park in 1935.

Earthquake Lake

ON Sunday night, August 16, 1959, actress Vicki Smith and a group of fellow Virginia City Players had the night off from performing at the Opera House. They were enjoying their rare free time by camping at nearby Ennis Lake. But there was something odd. Things had seemed off-kilter all day. The group had camped here many times, but the lake had never been so still and glasslike. There were no crickets singing in the night, no bugs flitting over the water, not a sound except the strange mooing of some nearby cattle. Vicki and her friends felt lethargic. Monday morning they packed up and left the lake, still wondering what felt so odd. Their questions were soon answered. The Monday evening performance had ended and the cast had assembled at a local bar for a nightcap. At 11:37, the

U.S. Geological Survey

Quake Mountain, showing the earthquake slide area that dammed the Madison River and created Earthquake Lake in August 1959.

elk's head on the wall suddenly tilted, and the ground shook. The street and wooden sidewalks undulated like waves. A 7.5 earthquake jolted the summer night, bringing worldwide attention to Montana and the West Yellowstone area. The worst of it hit the southern end of the Madison range near Hebgen Lake. The quake triggered a massive landslide that dammed the Madison River, creating Earthquake Lake. The earth bucked, heaved, and dropped, moved an entire mountain, fantastically tilted a lake, dumped sections of highway into it, and claimed the lives of twenty-nine people. The widespread temblors even destroyed a cell block at the Montana State Prison at Deer Lodge. The Forest Service has preserved and marked the quake-damaged area northwest of West Yellowstone. It is an event that Vicki Smith has never forgotten.

Dinosaur Trail

MONTANA'S vast, sparsely populated landscapes are rugged and scenic, but they also hold an ancient history. You can learn about Montana's incredible fossils by following the Dinosaur Trail. Start at Ekalaka where the Carter County Museum displays the complete skeleton of a duck-billed *Anatotitan copei,* one of five known specimens in the United States. The next stop, Makoshika State Park, was once home to at least ten species of dinosaurs and features unique, fossil-rich reddish panoramas aptly described as "hell cooked over." Museums at Glendive and Jordan, next along the trail, offer dinosaur digs and displays. Then visit the Fort Peck Interpretive Center to see the full-size cast of Peck's Rex, one of the most complete *Tyrannosaurus rex* skeletons yet discovered. Farther along the trail, the Phillips County Museum and the Dinosaur Field Station at Malta both welcome visitors. At the lab, you can see Leonardo, the famous mummified dinosaur, under preparation. Guinness World Records recognizes Leonardo as the best-preserved dinosaur. Havre's Clack Museum displays dinosaur eggs, and at

Harlowton, view a full-size replica of the first *Avaceratops* ever discovered. Museums at Choteau and Bynum highlight groundbreaking discoveries of baby dinosaur bones in Montana. Round out your trip with a visit to the Museum of the Rockies at Bozeman, laboratory of the renowned paleontologist and *Jurassic Park* film consultant Dr. Jack Horner. To learn more about Montana's Dinosaur Trail, explore the website at mtdinotrail.org.

Mining's Boom and Bust

A Fortune Almost Lost

NATE VESTAL purchased the Penobscot Mine near Silver City in Lewis and Clark County in 1877. He took nearly three hundred thousand dollars in gold ore from the mine. Vestal was not usually a gambling man, but sometimes he did like to play high-stakes poker. He was always good for a twenty when a friend needed a loan to keep a game going. Vestal would stake a friend, then sit tight and win it back, cleaning up the table. If he lost, he could afford it and would take it in stride. After one of his high-stakes wins, Vestal put his twelve-thousand-dollar winnings in a sturdy leather pouch and took the stage for Helena, intending to exchange his gold for cash at the U.S. Assay office. He tossed the leather pouch into the boot at the back of the stage. Upon arrival at the Paynes Hotel, which stood at the top of Sixth Avenue where the city-county building is today, Vestal got out of the Concord coach and made his way to the bar, never thinking about his gold. Friends greeted him warmly and took him into their circle. After several rounds of drinks, Vestal retired for the night. The next morning he suddenly remembered his pouch. Thinking he had left it with the desk clerk for safekeeping, he asked for it. It could not be found, and the stage, after a brief stop, had long departed. In a panic, Vestal ran out to the street and saw the pouch lying on the sidewalk. The driver had thrown it out, and Vestal's twelve-thousand-dollar fortune had been lying in plain sight all night long.

Millie Ringold's Enterprise

MILLIE RINGOLD was born a slave in Virginia in 1845. After emancipation, she traveled to Fort Benton as the nurse and servant of a U.S. Army general. He returned east, but Millie stayed and ran a boardinghouse. She learned of gold discoveries in the Judith Basin, and the excitement compelled her to sell her boardinghouse, buy two condemned army mules, provisions, and whiskey, and set out for Yogo City in 1878. She set up a hotel, restaurant, and saloon and for a couple of years mined the miners. But twenty years later, there was no gold left. Millie still set her tables with white linens even though she had no customers. Millie had some special talents. Miners claimed that she made the most beautiful music with mouth harps, band saws, washboards, and dishpans. She could make more music with an empty five-gallon can than most people could playing a piano. But Millie's burst of prosperity ended, and she eked out a meager living raising a few chickens and turkeys and prospecting for gold that she never found. She kept up hope that the town would rebound as the Hotel Ringold fell into decay. When finally rheumatism prevented Millie from driving her team and working her claims in 1903, Cascade County officials forced her to move to the county poor farm. But she was so unhappy there that they allowed her to return to Yogo City. Millie died destitute three years later and was buried in a piano crate in the cemetery at Utica.

Anaconda's Chinatown

CHINESE settlements and red-light districts were almost always adjacent for good reasons. Both prostitutes and Chinese were outcast populations, sometimes even confined by city ordinance to specific neighborhoods. Public women frequented the Chinese noodle parlors where meals were cheap and hearty, and they relied on Chinese herbalists and physicians for birth control and cures for venereal diseases, social issues that the mainstream medical community usually avoided. The proximity of Anaconda's Chinese settlement, however, was an exception. The Chinese were prominent in Anaconda's early community, settling about six blocks away from red-light activities. Chinese residents set up laundries, opened enterprising businesses, and worked in private households as domestics and cooks. In most Montana towns, such as Helena, Billings, and Missoula, the red-light district and the Chinese settlement would have grown toward each other. But this didn't happen in Anaconda. Not only did a city ordinance relocate Anaconda's red-light district, its four hundred Chinese residents quickly dwindled to just a few. Most moved on to settle in Butte's much larger district. This is partly because the Chinese competed with Anaconda's women in domestic and laundry services. Women in mining towns, especially in company towns like Anaconda where mining generated many widows, desperately needed to support their large families. Women's business opportunities were limited to keeping boardinghouses, taking in laundry, and working as maids or cooks for affluent families. These were the very occupations that engaged many Chinese. Although Anaconda was a company town, it sanctioned private enterprise for its women and effectively shut the Chinese out of business opportunities.

Castle

THE town of Castle in Meagher County was a wild camp where men died with their boots on. In the 1880s, two thousand residents rivaled the likes of the great camps of twenty years before. In the 1890s, the town's death was rapid as people left by the dozens. Their log cabins waited forlornly for owners to return and claim the household goods and belongings they left behind. But they never returned, and the buildings fell into decay. Two last residents kept up hope that the town would again come to life. Joseph Hooker Kidd and Joseph Martino were the last holdouts, optimistic that Castle would revive. In 1936, as Kidd and Martino wintered in their neighboring cabins, the snow piled up in drifts as deep as forty feet. The winter was extremely severe and supplies ran out. Kidd decided to go eight miles up the road to Lennep for groceries. By evening, his cutter and exhausted team had only gone three miles. He stayed the night at the Grande Ranch and the next day made it to Lennep. On the return trip, Kidd again shoveled drifts until he finally got within a mile of Castle. His team would go no farther so he turned them loose and set out on foot, reaching Martino's cabin late that evening. After some hot coffee, Kidd started out for his own cabin five hundred yards away. A few minutes later, Martino heard Kidd call out and saw him stagger. When Martino reached him, Kidd was dead. The population had been cut in half, its last resident left to foolishly dream that a great strike was still in Castle's future.

Meade Family Tragedies

DR. JOHN S. MEADE and his wife, Louisa, moved to Bannack in 1888 with their eight children. Dr. Meade remodeled the former Beaverhead County Courthouse, empty since 1881, as the Meade Hotel*. The courtroom and county headquarters became the lobby, parlors, and dining hall; the upstairs offices became bedrooms. Mrs. Meade set the tables with white linen, and good things came out of the kitchen at the back. One son, Perry, a graduate of the Colorado School of Mines, returned to Bannack in 1895 to work at the nearby Eugenia Mine. Perry and his wife, Lennie, had a new baby and needed the money. It was only his second shift, and Lennie did not like his working there. So when he kissed her goodbye, he said, "I'll find another job and I won't work underground after tonight."

It *was* Perry's last shift. A sea of mud flooded the tunnel. Hours later, workers found Perry with his face in the mud where he suffocated. Lennie went on with her life, raising her little son and helping her in-laws run the hotel. A year later, a measles epidemic struck Bannack. Dr. Meade and Louisa, a trained nurse who served in the Union army in the Civil War, tended the many sick children. They did everything they could for their grandson, but the little boy died. After these tragedies, the Meades had had enough of Montana. They moved to California, leaving the hotel to others. Perry and his little son, buried side by side in the Bannack cemetery, remind visitors that life back then was sometimes cruel.

Hydraulicking

PLACER gold is that which is loose in the soil and closest to the surface. Placer mining requires water to wash the dirt, perseverance, and a strong back. Gold is the heaviest material in the soil, and so in the process of washing, the heavy gold is the residue remaining in the pan or the sluice box. The rich goldfields that drew miners to Montana in the mid-1860s only held so much placer gold. Miners wanted to be sure to extract all of it, and so when that closest to the surface was depleted, they resorted to other methods of extraction. Hydraulic mining, or power washing, was one method. The Romans used a similar technique. They filled a reservoir or tank above the area to be flushed and allowed the water to flow down the hillside to expose the veins of gold. The first hydraulic mining in the West was done in California in 1853. Using a hose made of rawhide and a wooden nozzle to channel the water into elevated flumes, gravity created enough water pressure to move large rocks and boulders. Miners employed much the same method at Bannack, Alder Gulch, and Last Chance. They created a reservoir, then water wheels channeled water under tremendous pressure into huge hoses. These were then directed to the hillsides to power wash

Montana Historical Society Photograph Archives, Helena, Lot 26 B7 F6

Hydraulic placer mining, location and date unknown

the soil down to the bedrock. A series of sluices filtered the dirt. This destructive mining method drastically changed the landscape, reducing once-timbered hills to bare rock.

Aldridge

COAL veins discovered in 1892 in Park County fueled the life of Aldridge, a mining town about seven miles northwest of present-day Gardiner. Mostly Austrian immigrants, and a fair share of Italians, populated what briefly became one of the greatest coal producers in the country. By 1895, the mine's main entry had been driven 1,800 feet into the mountain. By 1897, the mines produced three to five hundred tons of coal daily for transport to the coke ovens 8,000 feet away. When the local miners organized a union that year on April 19, Montana Coal and Coke Company officials shut down the mines and coking plant, refusing to employ union men. But the workmen voted to stay with the union, and after several months, the company finally accepted a union contract. Aldridge became a strong union town with a union store and hospital with three staff doctors. The two most important holidays it celebrated were Union Day on April 19 and Labor Day. There were so many in Aldridge who could not speak English that the workmen were glad to have the union as their leader and spokesperson. The fortunes of the union thus became the fortunes of the camp. Progress came to Aldridge but helped spell its demise. Mules delivering the coal to the coke ovens were replaced by a flumed water system and later by an expensive electric tramway. Shortened shifts, shrinking workweeks, and inevitable strikes beleaguered the town. In 1910, the Montana Coal and Coke Company defaulted on bonds issued to pay for the tramway. Despite its rich veins, the mines closed and residents deserted Aldridge as quickly as they had come.

Cooke City

SOME years ago, eighty-eight-year-old Mrs. Ingeborg Reeb recalled life in the camp at Cooke City where her husband was a silver miner. She fondly remembered that even in the coldest, deepest winter, parties were frequent. Miners would come by the Reebs' place and each would take one of the Reebs' eight children under his arm—with legs dangling out the back—and head for the designated saloon. Pool tables pushed into the corners made comfortable and safe beds for the children. While they slept, the grownups danced. There was always plenty of coffee and wonderful food. Sometimes deep snow forced residents to move to lower elevations, and the Reebs would winter in Joliet. One spring as they returned to Cooke City, they traveled from Gardiner through Yellowstone and stopped to rest at Soda Butte. A troublesome rogue buffalo from the park's herd, dubbed "Old Johnson" in honor of the park superintendent, loved to terrorize humans. As the Reebs all jumped down from the buckboard, a man ran toward them shouting, "Get the children on the barn roof. Hurry. Old Johnson is coming!" Everyone raced to climb to the roof. Old Johnson came charging and buffaloed the family for two hours before finally giving up and wandering off. Sometimes, though, isolation in winter was grim. In 1914, the roads to Cooke City were impassable and snowmelt washed out the Lamar River Bridge. With no way in or out, a severe food shortage forced the community to survive on oatmeal for six weeks. But Mrs. Reeb recalled with nostalgia that despite bad times, the warmth of good neighbors bred the sweetest lifetime memories.

Neihart

NEIHART lies at the bottom of a densely timbered canyon along winding Highway 89. The tiny town traces its roots to 1881 when James Neihart and company discovered rich silver veins. By 1882, a crude wagon road connected it with White Sulfur Springs, and miners packed out the silver ore on horseback for processing at the Clendennin smelter twenty miles away. When the smelter shut down in 1883, ox-drawn freight wagons carried Neihart's ore to Fort Benton, where steamboats took it to distant ports. Even though the area was one of Montana's richest, lack of transportation hindered development. In 1891, a spur of the Montana Central Railroad linked Neihart with the outside world. The new smelter at Great Falls processed Neihart ore, and the town became the undisputed hub of the local mining district. Miners on payday flocked to the great mining camp to sample its saloons, play a game of cards, and visit the ladies in its several parlor houses. The bottom fell out of the silver market in 1893, but Neihart escaped the fate of most silver camps because its mines continued to sporadically operate. Total production of the Neihart mines up to 1900 included 4,008,000 ounces of silver and ten million pounds of lead. The 1940s saw the last burst of activity when silver prices briefly increased. By 1949, most mines closed permanently. The mines and mills, whose remnants still dot the hillsides, helped lay the cornerstones of Montana's economy. Six miles of underground tunnels lie beneath the hills surrounding Neihart. But today, above ground, it is tourism that boosts the local economy.

Rimini

JOHN CAPLICE discovered a rich vein in 1864 and soon local mines drew a solid population to this area. The early settlement, first known as Young Ireland, lay nestled in the shadow of Red Mountain's soaring 8,800-foot peak. In 1884, citizens petitioned for a post office, requesting the name of the town as Lee Mountain after the town's most important mine. But territorial governor Schuyler Crosby informed the delegation that the post office was not inclined to approve names of towns that had more than one word. The governor had just seen a production of the play *Francesca da Rimini* at Helena's Ming Opera House and loved it. He suggested the name Rimini, pronounced RIM-i-nee, after the Italian town of that name. But Irish miners assumed the name was Irish because Irishman Richard Barrett played the lead role. The post office was approved, but miners changed the pronunciation to RIM-in-eye and it stuck. Rimini boomed as the Northern Pacific Railroad's Rimini–Red Mountain branch line hauled gold, silver, lead, and zinc ore to the smelter at East Helena. Local mines generated some seven million dollars. The Hotel Rimini served delectable meals, and visitors from faraway places strolled along the main street. But mining waned, the post office closed in 1916, and train traffic ended in 1925. Mining remnants lie scattered everywhere. From 1942 to 1944, during World War II, remote Rimini was the U.S. Army's War Dog Reception and Training Center, where dogsled teams trained for search and rescue. Then the town became quiet. Today, picturesque Rimini is a patchwork of time periods and home to a handful of residents.

Kidnapped!

HARRY CHILD came to Montana in the early 1880s to learn the mining business from his uncle, wealthy investor A. J. Seligman. Child's vast interests eventually included mines and smelters, the Flying D Ranch in the Gallatin Valley, and Yellowstone Park's hotel and transportation companies. One of Child's many adventures has been recorded for posterity. Just before the Northern Pacific came to Helena in 1883, the two mining companies Child managed had stored their gold and silver bullion awaiting transport by rail. But the New York capitalists who financed the mining enterprises neglected the payroll and owed mine employees more than $125,000 in back pay. The son of one of these millionaire investors had come out to Montana to learn the mining business under Harry Child. The angry miners decided the fastest way to get their money was to kidnap Child and the millionaire's son. This they did and held the hostages in one of the mines. Child convinced the kidnappers to let him go to Helena to negotiate the ransom. Obtaining an open line through Western Union, Child succeeded in getting the money wired to Helena within twenty-four hours. Carrying the cash and fearful of bandits, Child made the hazardous twenty-five-mile trip by sleigh following a circuitous route. He later discovered that several parties of miners indeed had planned to rob him. Once paid, the miners returned to work. When the railroad finally came through, the first eastbound train out of Helena carried the gold and silver bullion to its investors, and everyone was satisfied.

A Miner's Lunch

AMONG the many ethnic groups that came to Butte were miners from Cornwall, England. These miners brought beliefs and traditions with them. They feared the Tommyknockers, who were the spirits of departed miners. Their ghostly knocking warned of cave-ins. Like all miners, the Cornish carried their lunches on their shifts underground. Terry Beaver of Helena has a collection of lunch boxes and has made a study of them. Often they were oval shaped and usually contained two inner trays, dividing the lunch pail into three separate compartments. The men poured their coffee in the bottom of the pail. The first tray fit over the coffee. This level contained a pasty, or meat pie. Made with bits of leftover meat and potatoes enclosed in a pastry envelope, this culinary staple had a tender nickname. Miners called it a "Letter from Home." A second tray on top of the pasty made the third and final level for pie or cake. The lid fit on top of it all, and a coffee cup fit on top of the lid. Miners would light a candle, stick it in the tunnel wall, and hang their lunch pails over the flame to heat their coffee and warm their pasty. Miners would never eat the crimped edges of the pasty. These they crumbled and dropped on the ground to pacify the Tommy-knockers and feed the rats that lived in the mines. The rats, they believed, deserved their respect and the miners took good care of them. Always present underground, rats sensed when a cave-in was imminent or if poison gas began to fill the tunnels. They would run out of the mine in droves, warning the miners of danger.

Modernizing Montana

Frontier Architecture

🞑 BANNACK, Virginia City, and Helena each had a turn as Montana's territorial capital, but each was destined for a different future. Today, Bannack is a state park whose empty buildings mostly date to the 1880s and later. Helena owes its survival beyond the mining phase to the Northern Pacific Railroad, which linked the town to distant markets in 1883. Few 1860s gold camp remnants survive in Helena. But Virginia City has a remarkable fifty-one 1860s gold rush–era buildings. Many of them show how frontier architecture was all about illusion. As the town transitioned from a temporary mining camp to a more permanent settlement, shopkeepers began to add false fronts to the log cabins. False fronts were architecturally important to mining camps because they made buildings seem taller, larger, and grander than they really were. This offered residents a sense of security in remote places like Alder Gulch. To the false fronts, shopkeepers began to add half-columns, arches, and medallions. These, crafted in wood on the frontier, mimicked the stone and brick ornamentation in the buildings of cities far away. Inside, muslin stretched smooth and tacked down over the rough log walls, gave the illusion of plaster. Wallpaper applied over the muslin made primitive interiors seem like tastefully decorated rooms. Virginia City's first substantial buildings, like Content's

Virginia City citizens pose near the corner of Jackson and Idaho Streets in the late 1860s.

Corner*, were of rubblestone. A layer of plaster scored to look like stone blocks covered the rough stones. The effect was dramatic. These surviving buildings and historic photographs of them give us a real sense of early residents' attempts at civilization.

Frank Lloyd Wright in Montana

IN 1991, the American Institute of Architects honored Frank Lloyd Wright as the Greatest American Architect of All Time. His theory of organic architecture held that structures should be in harmony with humanity and the human environment. When he died in 1959, he had designed over five hundred homes and structures in thirty-six states and Japan, Canada, and England. Some four hundred remain today. Montana claims several examples of his work, including one project from 1908 when Wright's career was just beginning to take off and another dating to the very end of his long architectural practice. The Como Orchards Colony, also known as the University Heights subdivision, in the Bitterroot Valley near

Darby was an experimental planned community. Wright came to Montana in 1908 to research the site and designed the Como Orchards as a summer refuge for university professors. A lodge and thirteen cottages were completed. One small cottage, a one-room cabin, and a tree-lined drive are all that remain today of Wright's experiment. It was an innovative idea and a very early use of the prairie style that made Wright famous. He also designed the Bitterroot Inn at Stevensville, but it burned to the ground in the 1920s. The Lockridge Medical Clinic in Whitefish, built in 1961, was one of Wright's last designs. Dr. T. L. Lockridge insisted on the building's construction even though his partners did not think it suitable as a medical clinic. For one thing, its hallways were too narrow for wheelchair access. When Lockridge died in 1964, his two partners moved elsewhere and sold the building. Now a law office, it is a surprising landmark in the middle of downtown Whitefish.

Montana Modernist

THE modernist style of architecture took wing in the United States in the 1950s and 1960s. Unlike any style before, modernist buildings made use of prefabricated elements of concrete, glass block, and metal. The streamlined appearance sought to humanize the industrialization of the early 1900s. Even though Montana's conservative small population inhibited large-scale modernist projects, some Montanans enthusiastically joined the movement. Eleven buildings on the campus of the University of Montana at Missoula, listed in the National Register of Historic Places, serve as great examples of modernist architecture in the state. Representing the time period between 1950 and 1963, they reflect the university's third period of expansion and convey the new aesthetics and exuberance of the mid-twentieth century. However, these stunning buildings also carefully conform to the planning efforts of two previous generations of campus architects. They have no classical columns or peaked roofs like the university's first buildings. Rather, architects intended these modernist structures to be viewed as sculpture with the surrounding landscape as part of the design. Contributing architects shared a vision that modernized the campus but respected the foresight of the two generations of architects before them. Carefully placed paths, sidewalks, and trees play as important a role as the walls and staircases of the buildings. Aerial views of the campus in the 1950s clearly illustrate the contrast between the dense picturesque earlier landscaping and the clean, linear effect of the grounds surrounding the modernist buildings. But the old and the new blend surprisingly well. Together they illustrate how a small neighborhood college evolved into a modern university with one of the most beautiful campuses in the West.

Davis Saddle

THERE were some five thousand African American buffalo soldiers who served in the all-black Ninth and Tenth Cavalry and Twenty-fourth and Twenty-fifth Infantry Regiments. Buffalo soldiers made up about 10 percent of the total troops who guarded the vast borders of the western frontier in the last quarter of the nineteenth century. These highly skilled, courageous, and patriotic soldiers served in Montana at forts throughout the state, including Fort Missoula, Fort Keogh, and Fort Assinniboine. In 1895, famed general "Black Jack" Pershing took his first command of the Tenth Cavalry, Troop H, at Fort Assinniboine. Pershing's men participated in a six-hundred-mile journey to flush Cree Indians out of the coulees and draws for their deportation to Canada. This grueling military expedition required patience and stamina, and Troop H accomplished it without the firing of a single shot. One of Pershing's men, William D. Davis, had a novel idea to make such long expeditions more comfortable. He invented a special type of improved saddle designed to render an easier ride on hard-trotting horses. Davis filed a patent on his improved saddle in 1896. His idea was to add springs beneath the seat and at the tops of the stirrups. While Davis did not invent the use of springs on saddles, the type of spring, its longevity, and its placement were his own. Although never standard army issue, Davis saddles provided a smoother ride for cavalry, cowboys, and gentlemen riders.

Electrification

THE first use of improved electric lighting occurred in 1879 when Thomas Edison lit his laboratory at Menlo Park, New Jersey, with an incandescent lighting system. Edison's genius, however, was not in the invention of the light bulb. Others had experimented successfully with incandescent lighting. Although Edison didn't really invent it, he did improve it. Most important, he developed a practical system that could be used in homes and businesses. It was a very complicated process that included many parts, and he was in competition with others also experimenting. He had to develop parallel circuits, an underground conductor network, a constant voltage, insulating material, an improved generator, and light sockets and switches. Edison came out ahead in the race. Once he had worked out all the parts, electric lighting spread quickly across the nation. Individual households and businesses had to supply their own bulbs and wiring. The community then had to purchase the generator and its accompanying steam engine and pay to operate them. The first systems could only supply electric lights to small areas, so communities had to have a series of generators and steam engines. The first electricity in Montana brought light to some of the mines in Butte by 1881. The first domestic electric light plants began providing service at Helena and Butte in 1882, only four years after Edison's system debuted. Plants at Billings, Great Falls, and Livingston provided services in 1887, plants at Bozeman by 1888, and plants at Missoula by 1889. In the next decade, electric lights shone from many homes, but only at night. It was not until the late 1890s that electricity became a twenty-four-hour service.

Fort Peck

PRESIDENT Franklin Roosevelt authorized construction of the Fort Peck Dam in 1933, beginning one of the nation's largest New Deal projects. The promise of work on the filled-earth dam brought as many as fifty thousand people to the area. Former college professors, hoboes, foreclosed farmers, and many others came from across the nation to help in the construction. The only thing they had in common was the need for work; the project employed nearly 10,500 men who had lost their livelihoods during the Great Depression. The townsite that sprang up to serve these instant

Montana Historical Society Photograph Archives, Helena, Fort Peck Dam Coll., B1, F7

President Franklin Roosevelt in his touring car at Fort Peck on October 3, 1937. With him are (from left to right) Montana governor Roy E. Ayers, Senator James E. Murray, district engineer Major Clark Kittrell, and an unidentified man.

residents was designed to be temporary. Instead, Fort Peck became a permanent community of about three hundred, and beautiful Fort Peck Lake is today a favorite recreation destination created from the 1930s Dust Bowl. Planners chose the Swiss chalet style, popularized in the national parks of the 1910s and 1920s, for the town's most prominent buildings, including the hospital, store, laboratory, Fort Peck Theater*, and Fort Peck Hotel*. While the theater offered entertainment to laborers and their families, the hotel catered to the many government employees and others who came to work, oversee, and inspect the building of the huge dam between 1933 and 1943. The hotel's rustic timbers, rough-sawn siding, and dramatic gabled entry became a permanent fixture in the temporary-turned-permanent townsite. The now privately operated hotel, refurbished to its 1933 ambience, is a community focal point and caters to visitors who come to enjoy this manmade paradise.

Safeway Stores

SOME Montanans might complain about box stores, but several large chain stores got their start before the beginning of the twentieth century. Sears, Roebuck & Co. and Woolworth were among the first. Grocery store chains took off in the first quarter of the twentieth century. Before 1910, customers typically purchased food on credit. They relied on clerks to fill their orders and on delivery boys to carry their packages home. By 1915, grocers began experimenting with a new model that offered lower prices and a wider selection to customers willing to serve themselves, pay cash, and forgo home delivery. Among the new stores was Safeway, whose name promoted the idea that paying cash was the "safe way to shop" because it kept families from going into debt. O. P. Skaggs Food Stores, which introduced its "efficient service system" and "cash and carry" policy, merged with Safeway, and the stores came to Montana in the 1920s. The first opened in Butte under the name

Skaggs-Safeway, and by 1931 most of the state's larger cities had Safeway stores. A debate over chain stores raged across the United States in the late 1920s. Small retailers and merchants led the anti-chain movement, and state lawmakers began passing anti-chain taxes. Montana was one of thirty-eight states to pass such legislation and one of twenty-two states whose tax law survived court challenges and referenda. That tax remains on Montana's books today, assessing chain stores at a graduated rate maxing out at a thirty-dollar annual charge for the eleventh store in a chain.

Bell Street Bridge*

THE Northern Pacific Railroad platted the townsite of Glendive in 1882 against the arid Montana "badlands" on the east side of the Yellowstone River. The location was an ideal supply and distribution center since it was where the railroad first met the Yellowstone, but Glendive looked to ranchers and farmers on the river's opposite side for economic support. After more than a decade of debate, the county erected the first bridge at Glendive in the mid-1890s. The four-span bridge included a swing span because the Yellowstone was still considered navigable. The bridge provided stockmen and farmers direct access to the railroad and made stage travel to points northwest much more reliable. In 1899, the bridge was washed out by a flood and ice jam. The Army Corps of Engineers had by then determined the Yellowstone unnavigable, and the bridge was rebuilt using one original span plus three new ones. It sufficed until better technology rendered the older structure obsolete. The new bridge, constructed between 1924 and 1926 with federal aid under the auspices of the Montana State Highway Commission, consists of six riveted Warren through trusses. This type of bridge construction is characterized by the W configuration made by its diagonal members and above-roadway trusswork. At 1,352 feet, the Bell Street Bridge is one of the longest of its kind in

Montana, representing a significant engineering accomplishment and an essential part of the area's commercial development.

Trains to Kalispell

As the tracks of the Great Northern Railway inched westward from St. Paul to Seattle, Flathead Valley towns vied for designation as the railway's division point. In spring 1891, however, railroad officials purchased land from the Reverend George Fisher and other early residents, founding a new settlement. The new town of Kalispell was platted in "T-town" form with Main Street perpendicular to one side of the proposed tracks. Some who doubted that the railroad would ever touch the new settlement dubbed it "Collapsetown" and "Wait a Spell," but even so lots sold for as much as $1,250. Construction boomed on Main Street with typical first-generation wooden-frame buildings, while many businesses were moved on log rollers four miles across the prairie from once-thriving Demersville, where steamboats ferried passengers across Flathead Lake. On New Year's Day 1892, the Great Northern Railway officially reached Kalispell. Banners proclaimed "Kalispell and St. Paul United by Steel," and the jubilant crowd noted that beer and whiskey were as free as the fresh air. Although the railroad moved its division point to Whitefish in 1904, Kalispell continued to prosper. Designated the county seat in 1893 and later bolstered by the homesteading era, the lumber industry, and tourism, Kalispell became an important trade, financial, and service center. Today, landmark buildings designed by architects Marion Riffo, Fred Brinkman, and George Shanley anchor the business district, but interspersed among them in greater numbers are the simple commercial buildings constructed by local masons and contractors. These form the true heart of the Main Street Commercial Historic District*, recalling the time when watering troughs, hitching rings, and wooden sidewalks lined the streets.

East Shore Road

CONVICTS at the Montana State Prison under controversial warden Frank Conley built five hundred miles of roads in counties across Montana during the 1910s. Other states also used convict labor, but the men were chained together under armed guards. Conley's honor system used no chains, and the guards carried no guns. The men lived in tents and did not wear the traditional striped prison clothing. Conley believed that self-respect was important and abolished the antiquated stripes intended to obliterate individuality. Inmates had to do some time without incident within the prison walls before they could work on the outside. The longer a man worked, the more he could reduce his sentence. Under Conley's system, the men accomplished tremendous amounts of work. One of the most difficult projects prisoners took on was the building of the East Shore Road at Flathead Lake. The twenty-seven-mile road was the longest stretch built by convict labor. Because there was no good road system, supplies for one of the two remote camps had to be shipped across the lake from Polson or Kalispell. More than one hundred prisoners worked on this backbreaking project, cutting through dense forest and blasting along the rocky shoreline. Although the men did have the use of pneumatic drills to break up the rocks, most of the work was done by hand with picks and shovels and teams of horses. Thirteen attempted to escape from the camps, but there were plenty of other prisoners to take their places. The road cost Flathead County $31,825 and is still in use, a testament to the excellent work done by convict laborers.

Index

Note: page numbers of entry titles appear in italics.

A. J. Gibson's Fatal Attraction, *173–74*
A River Runs Through It (book), *38–39*
Aaberg Cultural Resources, 96–97
Adams, J. C., 14
Adams, Louis, 84
Ainsworth, A. S., 51
Airey, Josephine "Chicago Joe," 53–54
Alder Gulch, 6, 21, 35, 144–45, 190, *1*
Aldridge, Montana, *191–92*
Allen, Arline, 78
Allen, Joseph, 78
American Fur Trading Company, 32, 104, 137, 168
Anaconda, Montana, 13, 111–12, 171, 187–88
Anaconda Saddle Club, *13*
Anaconda's Chinatown, *187–88*
Andrews, Sheriff Thomas, 49–50
Archie Bray Foundation, 12
Arline Allen's Embarrassing Innuendo, *78*
Army Nurse Corps, 132
Assiniboine Indians, 33, 97, 137, 158
August Heller's Saloon, *19–20*
Aviation History, *172–73*
Axline, Jon, 128–29
Ayers, Governor Roy, 103

Bad Boys, *82–83*
Bad Wound, 71
Baker, Jim, 30
Bangs, William, 62

Bannack, Montana, 79, 89, 99, 146–47, 153, 189–90, 190, 197
Bannack School, *89*
Basin, Montana, 129
Battle of the Little Big Horn, 35, 62, 74
Beachy, Hill, 37–38
Bear Paw Trail, *105–106*
Beattie brothers, 178
Beattie Park, *178*
Beaver Creek Park, 105–106
Beaverhead Rock, 98
Beaverhead Valley, 3
Begging Children, *81–82*
Bell, C. E., 46
Bell Street Bridge, *204–205*
Berry, Elizabeth Williams "Mother," *119*
Bicycle Corps, 130
Big Hole Battlefield, 98
Big Horn Gun, *157–58*
Big Man, Max, 181
Big Timber, Montana, 100
Bill Stockton's *Chief Joseph, 9–10*
Billings, Montana, 9, 17, 18, 23, 32–33, 39, 113–14, 154–55, 169, 201
Billings Townsite Historic District, *17*
Binks, Grace, photo of, 61
Birdseye, Clarence, 140
Bitterroot Valley, 4, 6, 25–26, 69, 84–85, 135, 140, 156–57, 160, 172
Blackfeet Indians, 6, 8, 30, 71, 137, 158, 168
Blackfeet Nation, 10

Boothill Cemetery (Billings), 39
Bootlegger Trail, *55–56*
Boulder Hot Springs, 98
Boulder, Montana, 6, 170–71
Bovey, Charles, 175
Bozeman, Montana, 28–29, 140,
 157–58, 185, 201
Brewster, Horace, 174
Bridger, Jim, 6
Bridgewater, Octavia, *132–33*
Brother Van's Love Story, *33–34*
Brown, Birdie (Bertie), *57–58*
Brucellosis, 139
Brush Lake, *177*
Buck (horse), 74–75
Buffalo and Brucellosis, *139*
Buffalo soldiers, 124–25, 130–31, 133,
 200–201; photo of, 130
Buffalo Soldiers in the Spanish-
 American War, *124–25*
Bullock, Seth, 45, 47–48
Butte Hangings, *162–63*
Butte, Montana, 5, 10, 14, 28, 40,
 43–44, 50–51, 56–57, 60, 98,
 162–63, 165–66, 201
Butts, Derinda Jane, 87–88

Calamity Jane, *see Canary, Martha*
Cameron, Evelyn, 64–65
Camp Paxson Boy Scout Camp,
 85–86
Campbell, J. L., 99
Canary, Martha, 80–81
Canyon Ferry, Montana 41–42
Capital Shenanigans, *45–46*
Capitol Commissions, *46*
Caplice, John, 194
Cardwell, Montana. 179
Carroll Trail, 108–109
Carsley, George, 12
Cascade, Montana, 175
Case, Joseph "Fisher Jack," 62
Cashman Quarry, 98
Castle, Montana, *188–89*
Castle, The, *22*
Cats Earned Their Keep, *69*
Cedar Creek, 101
Cemetery Island, *41–42*

Central Park, *176–77*
Charlie Russell's Hearse, *174–75*
Charlo, 5, 6
Cheadle, Larry, 121–22
Chicago, Burlington, and Quincy
 Railroad, 17
Chief Joseph (sculpture), 9
Chief Plenty Coups Memorial State
 Park, 111
Child, Harry, 119, 195
Child, W. C., 2
Children in the Mining Camps,
 77–78
China Gulch, 101
Chinese, 4, 14, 100–101, 102, 187–88
Chinese in Big Timber, *100*
Chinese Settlements, *101–102*
Chippewa (steamboat), 167–68
Chippewa-Cree Indians, 158
Christmas, 147–149, 150–51
Christmas at the Rio, *150–51*
Civil War, 125, 144, 145, 178, 190
Civil War Vets, *125*
Clark, Florence, *111–12*
Clark, William A., 28
Clark, William, 32, 169
Clark Fork River, 18, 27
Clarke, John L., *6–7*
Clarke, Malcolm, 6
Colby, Edith, 51–52; photo of, 52
Coleman, Philip J., Jr., 52–53
Colter, John, 30
Combs, Mary Ann, *84–85*
Conley, Frank, 120–21, 206
Connor, Linnie, 138
Conrad Cemetery, *42–43*
Conrad Family, 24–25, 42
Conrad Mansion, *24–25*
Cooke City, Montana, *192–93*
Cooley, Dr. Robert, 140
Copper King Mansion, *28*
Coulson, Montana, *39*
Cowboy and His Horse, A, *74–75*
Cowboy, The (painting), 6
Cree Indians, 98
Crow Agency Archaeology, *96–97*
Crow Indians, 4, 8, 33, 70, 104, 108,
 111

Crump, James Wesley, 125
Curiosity, A, 99
Custer, General George, 35, 62, 73–74
Custer's Dogs, 73–74
Custer's Last Stand (painting), 5

Daly Mansion, 25–26, 173
Daly, Marcus, 13, 25
Daly, Margaret, 25–26
Darby, Montana, 156, 199
Davis Saddle, 200–201
Davis, William D., 200–201
Davey, Frank, 82–83
Deadwood (television series), 47
Dean, Maria, 90
DeCamp, Ralph, 3
Deer Lodge Valley, 98, 147
Deer Lodge, Montana, 49, 91–92
Demise of the York Block, 43–44
DeSmet, Pierre Jean, 135
DHS Ranch, 2
Diamond City, Montana, 22
Dillon, Montana, 10, 34, 165
Dimsdale, Thomas, 79
Dinosaur Trail, 184–85
Dixon, Cromwell, 172–73; photo of, 172
Dorman, Isaiah, 35
Driving the Golden Spike, 4
Drouillard, George, 32
Dwyer, Terry, 38
Dynamite (dog), 70

Eagle's Store, 181–82
Earthquake Lake, 183–84; photo of, 183
East Glacier, Montana, 7
East Helena, 2
East Shore Road, 206
Edgar, Henry, 6
Edgerton, Henry, 147
Edgington, Reverend Robert, 68
Edith Colby's Mistake, 51–52
Eisenhower, Dwight D., 126
Eitner, Paul "Turkey Pete," 122–23
Eklaka, Montana, 184
Electrification, 201–202

Elk Head, 9
Elling, Henry. 107
Ellingsen, John, 106
Ellis Family's Wagon, The, 65–66
Ely, Eugene, 172–73
Emanuel, Bertram, 30
Evelyn Cameron Scandalizes Miles City, 64–65
Expensive Cats, 72

Farmer, Almeda, photo of, 83
Farmer, Winnifred, photo of, 83
Feldberg, Jacob, 116
Fergus County, 57
First Female at Deer Lodge, 49–50
First Missoula Cemetery, 31
First Montana Christmas, 147–48
Fisher, Bessie, 50–51
Flathead Valley, 13, 41, 84
Flatheads Leaving Their Bitterroot Home, The (painting), 5
Fletcher, Robert, 180
Fort Assinniboine, 105–106, 124, 133, 200
Fort Benton, Montana, 14, 72–73
Fort Ellis, 157
Fort Keogh, 200
Fort Missoula, 124, 126–28, 172, 200
Fort Missoula Historical Museum, 53
Fort Missoula Internees, 126–28, photo of, 127
Fort Peck, 202–203; photo of, 202
Fortune Almost Lost, A, 186–87
Frank Lloyd Wright in Montana, 198–99
Frenchtown, Montana, 40–41
Frontier Architecture, 197–98; photo of, 198
Frontier Holiday Fare, 146
Frye, "Big Eva," 50
Fuller, Miles, 162–163

Gallows Barn, 48–49
Gardiner, Montana, 191
Garnet, Montana, 82, 83, 84
Gates of the Mountains, 3
George Drouillard's Luck Runs Out, 32

German Gulch, 102
Ghost Horse Named Paint, The, 70–72
Gibson, A. J., 25, 26, 173–74
Gilbert, Cass, 12
Glacier National Park, 18
Glendive, Montana, 16–17, 102, 104, 118, 184, 204, 204
Gold Creek, 4
Gold Fever, 79
Gordon Family, 115
Gordon, Taylor, 115
Gore, Sir George, 104
Gormley, Julia, 144–45
Grant, Kirby, 112–13
Grant, Ulysses S., 4
Grant-Kohrs Ranch, 98
Great Falls, Montana, 93–94, 133, 134, 152–53, 175, 193, 201
Great Northern Railway, 7, 10, 17, 171, 205
Greenough Mansion, 26–27; photo of, 27
Greenough, Thomas L., 18, 26
Gros Ventre Indians, 7, 97, 158
Ground Observer Corps, 128–29

Hagan Site, 18
Haire, C. S., 28
Hamilton, Montana, 141, 173
Hansen, Kay, 9
Hanukkah, 154–55
Hard Winter, 2–3
Harlowton, Montana, 185
Haughian, Henry, 74, 75
Hauser, Samuel, 170
Havre, Montana, 105, 184
Helena, Montana, 12, 23–24, 38, 47–48, 53–54, 91, 116–17, 125, 126, 138, 145, 150, 154, 161–62, 172–73, 178, 194, 197, 201
Helena's Paul Revere, 116
Hell Gate, Montana, 167, 166
Heller, August, 19–20
Hickman, R. O., 45
Higgins, C. P., 67, 167
Hilger, Margaret, 2
Hill, James J., 171

Hill, Louis Jr., 171
Hillen, Father Dan, 162
Homestead Act, 59–60
Homestead Horror! 66
Horner, Dr. Jack, 185
Hosmer, J. Allen, 80
House of the Good Shepherd, 138
Hunter, Moses, 125
Hurdy-Gurdy Houses, 53–54
Hydraulicking, 190–91; photo of, 191

Independence Day in Alder Gulch, 144–45
Indian Boarding Schools, 88–89
Indian Chief, The (painting), 6
Industrial Workers of the World (IWW), 40
Ingalls, Emma, 91
Inverness, Montana, 62
Irish, 4
Isaiah Dorman, "Black White Man," 35
Ismay Jail, 15–16
Ismay, Montana, 15–16

J. C. Adams Stone Barn, 14
James J. Hill's Legacy, 171
Jack Slade's Funeral, 36–37
Japanese Americans, 126–27
Japanese Balloons, 129
Jocko Reservation, 6
John Colter's Ghost, 30–31
Johnston, Jennie, 33–34
Joliet, Montana, 165
Jordan, Montana, 184
Josephine conquers the Yellowstone, The, 168–69
Joullin, Amédeé, 4
Judith River Ranger Station, 178–79

Kalispell, Montana, 19–20, 24, 42–43, 129, 205
Kaufman, Louis, 2
Kelley, Tom, 49
Kennedy, John F., 13
Kent, J. H., 46
Kenyon, Virginia Geiger, 142–43
Kidd, Joseph Hooker, 189

Kidnapped! *195*
Kleffner Ranch, 2
Kootenai Indians, 156
Kristoffersen, Arvid, 25

LaHood Park, *179–80*
Largey, Patrick, 107–108
Larpenteur, Charles, 137
Last Chance Gulch, 190
Last of the 5,000 (sketch), 2
Laugh Kills Lonesome (painting), *1–2;*
    reproduction of, viii
Laugh Kills Lonesome (song), 1–2
Laurel Roadside Museum, *180–81*
Laurin, Adaline, 119–20
Laurin, Jean Baptiste, *119–20*
Laurin, Montana, 119–20
Lawrence, Mary, 165–66
Ledger Art, *8–9*
Legal Beer, *56–57*
Legend of the Bitterroot, *160–61*
Lesson on the Trail, A, *87–88*
Lewis and Clark Caverns, 179, *182*
Lewis and Clark County Courthouse,
    48
Lewis, Meriwether, 18, 160
Lewis, Oscar T., 102, 103, *118–19*
Lincoln County Ferry Goes
    A.W.O.L., *169–70*
Little, Frank, 40
Little Rocky Mountains, *158–59;*
    photo of, 159
Livingston, Montana, 65, 201
Lloyd Magruder's Grisly End, *37–38*
Lochrie, Elizabeth, *10*
Logan, Mike, 1
Lolo, Montana, 141
Long Horse, 108
Lynching of Frank Little, 40

M, The *94–95*, photo of, 94
MacHaffie Site, 98
Maclean, Norman, 38–39
Maclean, Paul, 38–39
Madison Valley, 36
Magruder, Lloyd, 37–38
Majors, Margaret, photo of, 61
Malta, Montana, 184

Mammoth Meadows, 98
Manire, John, 51
Manlove, Jonathan and Almira,
    60–61
Mansfield, Senator Mike, 127
Mares, Frank and Joseph, 176–77
Mariana, Nick, 134
Marsh, Captain Grant, 168–69
Martino, Joseph, 189
Masons, 89
Mayhew, H.H., *170–71*
McCray, Dr. Arthur, 141
Meade, Dr. John S., 189, 190
Meade Family Tragedies, *189–90*
Medicine Crow, Joe, 33
Medicine Rocks State Park, *97–98*
Medicine Tree, *156–57*
Melrose, Montana, 148
Merrill Avenue Historic District,
    16–17
Miles City, Montana, 16, 54, 64, 74,
    90, 122, 125, 148
Miles City Christmas 1884, *148–49*
Miller, James Knox Polk, 21
Millie Ringold's Enterprise, *187*
Miner's Lunch, A, *195–96*
Mining Camp New Year's, *153–54*
Mining Camp Thanksgiving,
    146–47
Missoula Cemetery, 31
Missoula County Courthouse, 5
Missoula, Montana, 5, 18, 26, 31, 38,
    49, 52, 67, 95, 130–31, 167, 171,
    172, 199–200, 201; photo of, 94
Missoula's Garden Roots, 67
Missouri Fur Company, 32
Montana Central Railroad, 193
Montana Historical Society, vii, 9,
    10, 12, 83
Montana Modernist, *199–200*
Montana State Capitol, 3, 4, 5, 28,
    46, 47, 60, 64, 135
Montana State Hospital at Galen, 10
Montana State Prison, 50–51, 54–55,
    86, 120–23, 184, 206
Montana State School, 90
Montana Territorial Prison, 9, 49, 5
Montana's First Condo, *106–107*

Montana's First Doctor, *135–37*
Montana's Last Hanging, *52–53*
Montana's National Historic
    Landmarks, *18–19*
Montana's Second Book, *79–80*
Monte (horse), *70–72*; photo of, 71
Morgan, Annie, *62–63*
Morrison, Dan, 182
Moss, Lieutenant James, 131
Moss, Preston, 23
Moss Mansion, *23*
Mountain View School for Girls,
    90–91
Mullan Road, 18, *40–41*, 92, 167
Mulloy, Dr. William, 103, 118
Murphy, Muriel, *86*
Myers, Thomas Guy, *178*

Nancy Wright's Sacrifice, *35–36*
Nation, Carry, 20
National Historic Landmarks, *18–19*
National Register of Historic Places,
    11–12
Naval Ships, *126*
Neihart, Montana, *193–94*
Nesmith, Michael, 1
Nevada City, Montana, 49, 81
New Year, *151–54*
New Year's Folklore and Traditions,
    151–52
New Year's in 1913, *152–53*
Newman, William, 86
News from the States (mural), 10
Nez Perce Indians, 9, 98, 109
Nez Perce Pass, 37
Nihill, Montana, 48
Norris, Governor Edwin, 140
Northern Cheyenne Indians, 88, 97
Northern Pacific Railroad, 3, 4, 16,
    17, 18, 35, 39, 157, 167, 170, 171,
    178, 182, 204
Not in Our Town, *154–55*

O'Brien, Thomas, *120–21*
O'Keefe, Baron, *45–46*
Old Man Stormit, *163–64*
Old-time dances, *63–64*
Olinghouse, E., 106

Original Governor's Mansion, *23–24*
Owens, Kenneth and Sally, 139

Paint (horse), *see Monte*
Painted Tipis, *7–8*
Paris Gibson Junior High Blows Up,
    93–94
Paris Gibson Square, 94
Parker, Dr. Ralph, 141
Paul Maclean's Unsolved Murder,
    38–39
Paulsen, John C., 46, 90
Paxson, Edgar S., 3, *4–5*, 86
Pedretti brothers, 5
Pekin Noodle Parlor, *14–15*
Philipsburg, Montana, 62
Pictograph Cave, 18, *102–103*, 180;
    photo of, 103
Pictograph Cave Cannibals, *102–103*
Piper, Helen C., photo of, 117
Place Where the White Horse Went
    Down, *32–33*
Placer Hotel, *12–13*
Plassman, Martha Edgerton, *153–54*
Plenty Coups, Chief, 18, *111*; photo
    of, 110
Plentywood, Montana, 66, *114–15*, 177
Plummer, Henry, *109*, 147
Poacher Gulch, *100–101*
Pompey's Pillar, *169*
Potts, Territorial governor Benjamin,
    50
Prescott, Clarence, 65
Prison Escape, *120–21*
Prohibition, *55–56*, *57–58*, 177
Prospector, The (painting), 6
Pryor, Montana, 18

Ralston, J. K., 6
Rattlesnake, The, *18*
Ravalli, Father Anthony, 69, *135–36*
Red Whip, 158
Reeb, Mrs. Ingeborg, *192–93*
Reed and Bowles, *108–109*
Reeves, "Daddy," *116–17*, photo of,
    117
Remnants of Native Culture in
    Southwestern Montana, *98–99*

Ricketts, Dr. Howard, 139
Rimini, Montana, *194*
Ringold, Millie, 187
Rio Theater, 150–51; photo of, 151
Rockfellow House, *21–22*
Rocky Mountain Laboratory, *140–41*
Rocky Mountain spotted fever,
  139–40
Ronan, Mary, 36–37
Roosevelt, Franklin, 180; photo of,
  202
Roosevelt, Theodore, 124–25, 131,
  182
Roping a Coyote (painting), 118
Ross, Alexander, 156
Russell, Charles Marion, 1, 2, 3, 4, 6,
  12, 71, 118, 174–75; photo of, 71
Ruth, Harold, 114
Ryegate, Montana, 53

Safe Crossing, *167*
Safeway Stores, *203–204*
St. Helena Cathedral, 161–62
St. Mary's Mission, 69, 137; photo
  of, *136*
St. Peters (steamboat), 137
St. Regis, Montana, 166
Salish Indians, 5, 18, 84–85, 135–36,
  161
Sanchez, Felicita, *49–50*
Sanders, Harriet, 72, 79, 144,
  146–47
Sanders, Mingo, *131–32*
Sanders, Wilbur, 45, 79, 146
Sayle, Montana, 54
Sayre, Melville, 102–103, 118
Schanche, Tony, 73
Schnitzer, Isaac, 154–55
Sedition, *54–55*
Seth Bullock and the First Legal
  Hanging, *47–48*
Seventh Legislative Session, 47
Sheehan, Mary "Mollie," 79, 144,
Shep (dog), *72–73*
Sherman, Byron R., 22
Shope, Irvin "Shorty," 180
Shopping 1896, *149–150*
Sigma Alpha Epsilon, 29

Singing Voice, 7
Sioux Indians, 35, 97, 158
Skunk Whiskey, *56*
Skunkwagons, *175*
Sky King, 112–13
Slade, Jack, 36–37
Slade, Virginia, 36–37
Sleeping Child Hot Springs, *160*
Smalley, Laura Etta, *61–62*
Smallpox Vaccine, *137–38*
Smith, Elizabeth Farmer, 83–84;
  photo of, 83
Smith, Governor Robert B., 46
Smith, Janet, 54, 55
Smith, Vicki, 183–84
Smith, William, 54, 55
Smith River Valley, 22
Smoking Cure, *80*
Snyder, Jean Maclean, 39
Solitary Confinement, *121–22*
Spanish-American War, 5, *124–25*, 131
Speculator Mine, 40
Spencer, Dr. Roscoe, 141
Stadler, Louis, 2
Stagecoach Tips, *166*
Stained Glass Artistry, *161–62*
Stanfel, Jane, 58
State Capitol Rotunda Roundels, *5–6*
Steamer *Chippewa, 167–68*
Stevens, Governor Isaac, 166
Stevensville, Montana, 69, 135, 199
Stewart, Governor Samuel, *24*, 49
Stoner, Julius, 173
Stoner Transportation Company, *173*
Stormit, J. P., *163–64*
Story, Thomas Byron, 28–29
Stuart, Granville, 2, 45, 147
Student Nurse, *142–43*
Summers in Garnet, *83–84*
Summit, Montana, 36
Sun River, 14
Superior, Montana, 92, 93
Superior School Building, *92–93*

T. Byron Story Mansion, *28–29*
Taylor, Franci, 88
Taylor, Jack, 125
Teenage Troubles, *138*

Thanksgiving, 145, 146–47
Thanksgiving in December, *145*
Thomas, Homer, *76–77*
Thompson Falls, Montana, 51–52
Those Old-time Dances, *63–64*
Three Forks of the Missouri, 30, 32
Titanic Memory, *165–66*
Toole, Governor Joseph K., 4, 5, 6
Trail of Destruction, *104*
Trails and Trials (book), 80
Train Wreck at Boulder, *170–71*
Trains to Kalispell, *205*
Trapper, The (painting), 5
Trask Hall, *91–92*
Trip to the States, A (book), 79–80
Troy, Montana, 169–70
Tuck (dog), 74
Turkey Pete, *122–23*
Twenty-fifth Infantry Bicycle Corps,
    130–31; photo of, 130

UFOs, *134*
Ultimate Service, *133*
Unsanitary Public Places, *141–42*
USS *Helena,* 126
USS *Missoula,* 126
USS *Montana,* 126
USS *Montanan,* 126
Utica, 2, 178, 187

Van Orsdel, William Wesley
    "Brother Van," 33–34; photo of, 34
Verendrye, Pierre Gaultier de
    Varennes, Sieur de la, 104, 105
Verendryes, The, *104–105*
Vestal, Nate, 186, 187
Victor, Montana, 128
Vigilantes of Montana (book), 79
Villard, Henry, 4
Vindex, Charles, 114–15
Vindex Family's Hard Times, *114–15*
Virginia City, Montana, 11, 21–22, 37,
    45–46, 72, 79–82, 87, 106–107,
    125, 144–45, 145, 153, 183–84,
    197–98; photo of, 198

Waiting for a Chinook (sketch), 2
Walkers Bar, 56–57
War against Ticks, *139–40*
Warden, Mr. and Mrs. Tyler, 141
Warren, Olive, *113–14*
Watson, Clell, 47
Weeping Child, 160
Wegars, Priscilla, 101
West Yellowstone, Montana, 181–82,
    184
Wheatley, 48
Wheeler, Burton K., 40, 51
White, Colonel Almond, 68
White Sulphur Springs, Montana,
    22, 48–49, 115, 193
Whitefish, Montana, 199, 205
Wild Horse Island, *68–69*
Williams, Lyle, 56
Winburn, Roy, 133
Wooden Leg, 74
Worden, Francs (Frank), 165, 166
Work, Clemens P., 54
World War I, 29, 40, 54, 126, 133
World War II, 13, 23, 40, 126,
    128–29, 132, 141, 184
Wright, Frank Lloyd, 198–99
Wright, Nancy Millsop, 35–36

Yeager, Eileen, 80–81
Yeager, Mary, 80–81
Yellowstone National Park, 3, 65,
    192; photo of, 130
Yellowstone Valley, 39, 104
Yogo City, Montana, 187
York Block, 43–44
Yow, Hum, 15

Zettler, F. X., 161, 162